Classroom Routines for Real Learning

Daily management exercises that empower and engage students

JENNIFER HARPER

KATHRYN O'BRIEN

Pembroke Publishers Limited

To our current students for allowing us to learn and grow with you; for testing, breaking, and rediscovering routines on our learning curve. — Jen and Kathryn

To Casey for his love, and to Dean, Jack, and Bret, my buddy authors, who continually remind me why routines are so necessary. — Jen

To Dave for teaching me (with love) the importance of uni-tasking, and to Samuel for constantly reminding me that routines need to be fun and meaningful, and occasionally need to be broken. — Kathryn

© 2015 Pembroke Publishers
538 Hood Road
Markham, Ontario, Canada L3R 3K9
www.pembrokepublishers.com

Distributed in the U.S. by Stenhouse Publishers
480 Congress Street
Portland, ME 04101
www.stenhouse.com

We acknowledge the financial support of the Government of Canada through the Canada Book Fund (CBF) for our publishing activities.

We acknowledge the assistance of the Government of Ontario through the Ontario Media Development Corporation's Ontario Book Initiative.

Library and Archives Canada Cataloguing in Publication

Harper, Jennifer, author
    Classroom routines for real learning : daily management exercises that empower and engage students / Jennifer Harper, Kathryn O'Brien.

Includes index.
Issued in print and electronic formats.
ISBN 978-1-55138-297-5 (pbk.).--ISBN 978-1-55138-906-6 (pdf)

    1. Classroom management. I. O'Brien, Kathryn, 1974-, author II. Title.

LB3013.H37   2015   371.102'4   C2014-907878-1
                                          C2014-907879-X

Editor: Kat Mototsune
Cover Design: John Zehethofer
Typesetting: Jay Tee Graphics Ltd.

Printed and bound in Canada
9 8 7 6 5 4 3 2 1

FSC
www.fsc.org
MIX
Paper from
responsible sources
FSC® C004071

Contents

Introduction

> "We are what we repeatedly do. Excellence, therefore, is not an act but a habit."
>
> Aristotle

We all have routines. Even those among us who say they despise routines have routines. The coffee in the morning, the laying out of clothes the night before, the route we drive to school, the way we organize our photocopies—they are all routines.

As an educator, it is a conundrum. The essence of our teaching is trying to empower and engage our students; yet here we are, discussing what is arguably the most traditional, teacher-directed element of school—routines. Routines are rules. They are the sequence and the order that students are asked to follow—be it walking in line down the hall, raising hands to sharpen pencils, or answering when their names are called for attendance. Established routines run themselves, they are the well-oiled machines that can make a classroom function. They are the backbone of our teaching practice. And typically, they are the most teacher-directed part of any school day.

So why take time to ponder the professional routines in our classrooms? Because we need to rethink what routines we use and how those routines affect our students. We want routines to run smoothly and to be effective. And we want to model that efficiency. However, we also want our students to feel empowered, motivated, and engaged during even the most mundane classroom routine.

In our last book, *Student-Driven Learning*, we wrote about creating a framework for developing a classroom that fosters inquiry-based student-centric learning. This book continues as an extension of our first; how can we use routines to create more students who are willing to take risks, be creative, think critically, and be more resilient, self-regulated, curious, and empathic? We realized that we needed to redefine the concept of routines and explore how we use routines within our classrooms in ways that engage students.

To write this book, we began with backward design (thanks to Wiggins & McTighe) and thought about our role as educators. We wanted to have a framework for what we do within our schools, so we began with *What is expected of us?* Here's what we came up with:

- Curriculum expectations
- Academic progress for each student
- Communication with the school community

With these factors in place, we asked ourselves the most important question: *What do we want for our students?*

- Empathy: We want our students to be able to relate to others through various perspectives. We want them to be emotionally sensitive with kind and generous hearts toward others.
- Curiosity: We want students to wonder, ask questions, and investigate.
- Creativity: We want students to be adventurous, to build, experiment, create, and try out various techniques and strategies.

- Critical thinking: We want students to seek the answers to their questions, to connect what they find, sort it, rank it, and prioritize key points, and to come out with a richer understanding.
- Motivation: We want students to be passionate about learning and to be trying their best. We want them to be driven internally.
- Resilience: We want students to feel free to make mistakes and then learn from them. We want them to bounce back, knowing that mistakes are essential for learning.
- Self-regulation: We want students to be mindful of themselves, their space, and their interactions with others. We want them to foster their own independence.

We would like all this for each student; moreover, we feel that these concepts are essential for them to navigate and embrace their learning.

How do routines fit within this list? How do we use routines to provide what we want for our students? We began to think about how we could foster and develop what we want for our students within the expectations of our teaching role. Where can we fit in the big concepts? Where do we squeeze in empathy? Or critical thinking? When do we teach our students to be resilient or self-regulated? How do we find time to communicate with parents? To share ideas with colleagues? Where do we find those teachable moments to solidify curriculum goals?

As we thought about these questions, we realized that routines provide the opportunity to meet our professional obligations and to create a learning environment that cultivates student-driven learning. We realized that even the most mundane of routines, such as collecting homework, can be a chance to develop accountability and motivation in our students. Our school day is filled with routines. These routines—arriving in class, taking attendance, handing in homework, sharpening pencils, moving through the hallways, recess, lunch—are an essential part of every school day and every childhood. Thoughtfully implemented and used, routines can build classroom community, foster independent work, and encourage collaboration.

This book is designed as a bank of learning experiences, instructions, tips, ideas, and strategies for everyday classroom routines. We developed, collected, and experimented with routines to help you establish routines as the building blocks of dynamic classrooms, where students are engaged, empowered, and independent in their learning.

Our routines are written to follow you through a typical teaching day. After sharing strategies to establish routines in Chapter 1, Chapter 2 focuses on morning routines and getting students into the classroom, where they are set up for success. Chapter 3 includes routines that help foster a caring classroom and build a classroom community; Chapter 4 focuses on routines for independent work and helping students improve their executive functioning skills; Chapter 5 presents a bank of routines around collaborative work; routines in Chapter 6 focus on assessment. Finally, Chapter 7 routines end the school day, and Chapter 8 looks at routines that extend beyond the classroom walls.

This book offers a variety of routines you can use and modify as you like: in the fresh start of the year; at the bump a few months in, when routines need tweaking; to restart after the mid-year break when order needs to be reestablished; and all the way to the end of the school year, when we need new tricks to get our students scrambling to the finish line.

CHAPTER 1

Establishing Routines

"We all have our routines," he said softly. "But they must have a purpose and provide an outcome that we can see and take some comfort from, or else they have no use at all. Without that, they are like the endless pacing of a caged animal. If they are not madness itself, then they are a prelude to it."

John Connolly, *The Book of Lost Things*

Routines by definition are humdrum things. As an adjective, the word *routine* is synonymous with *average, common, unexceptional, unremarkable, garden-variety...* You get the idea. In an age that values diversity, creativity, and excitement, routines can appear to be the antithesis of engagement and motivation. But anyone who works in an environment that depends on organization and collaboration with others will tell you that routines are essential to providing order. Not all routines are positive, though. As educators, we need to examine the nature of the routines we use and reflect on their purpose and efficacy within our classrooms.

What Is a Routine?

A routine is an established procedure for completing a task. The procedure is used consistently and becomes an innate process. While they are more flexible than rules, routines or procedures are specific ways of doing things that, for the most part, vary little during the course of the day and persist over an extended time period. Classrooms typically require many routines to operate efficiently and effectively (McLeod et al., 2003). For example, routines commonly include how to enter and leave the classroom, take attendance, indicate lunch selection, secure materials, dispose of trash, label work, turn in assignments, make a transition during or between instructional activities, get to safety during drills and actual emergencies, and change from one activity or location to another (Stronge, Tucker & Hindman, 2004). In essence, routines shape the classroom climate. Teachers and students follow the process because it creates order and stability.

How can procedures and routines help maximize learning? By providing the following:

- Stability: Everyone knows what to expect and feels comfortable knowing what to do to be successful.
- Consistency: Everyone can anticipate what lies ahead, and with this anticipation can make plans and set goals.

- Time management: When effective routines are in place, students can complete daily tasks with greater independence and less adult intervention. In turn, teachers have more time available to work one-on-one and in small groups.

Routines and Rituals

In researching this book about routines, we came across many amazing rituals in classrooms. A routine, the steps we complete to get a task done, is functional. A ritual, like a routine, has a series of steps, but there is greater meaning attached the actions. Rituals tend to be experiences that are repeated from year to year. Rituals take place around birthdays, end-of-year activities, receiving awards, and other special events we celebrate and honor. It is these rituals that students tend to remember years later, and rituals often define their memories from the classroom.

Redefining Routines

Routines have value. They help our students feel stable and successful; they create a sense of knowing in the classroom environment. Consistent routines can allow for more time for class learning and can provide expectations for students to follow. Like any classroom interaction, routines can glide on the continuum of responsibility. They can be created, directed, and maintained by the teacher or they can be entirely created, directed, and maintained by students—or any place in between (see sample continuum below).

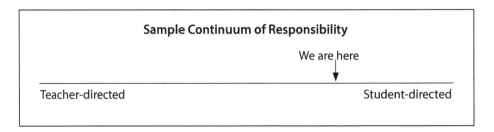

If a teacher has initiated the tasks that need to be done in the classroom and has provided explicit teaching around the tasks, the routines will likely be successful. But will students be engaged in their own learning? Likely not. Routines that are entirely teacher-directed offer extrinsic motivation, like the carrot and the stick: students perform the task with the hope of a "well done" or other positive feedback. On the other side of the continuum, if a teacher creates a classroom in which students help identify tasks that are valuable and important, are students more inclined to respect the routines? Yes. And by modelling and engaging children in classroom routines, we are also modelling behavior that can create positive habits outside the classroom. We empower students with the tasks so that they embrace the routine. We are providing them intrinsic motivation.

The move toward differentiated classrooms encourages teachers to be more flexible and in tune with the individual needs of their students. If we can shake our perception of routines as rigid and teacher-based, and work to implement engaging and student-focused routines, we will actually create a more student-driven learning environment.

What are the roles of routines in today's differentiated classroom?

- Increasing active student engagement through individual accountability
- Establishing a positive classroom climate by making students understand how their effort helps the classroom run
- Creating a sense of self-regulation among students
- Establishing task expectations that can be completed with little or no teacher guidance

Unravelling Routines

In the quote on page 7, the Woodsman in John Connolly's *The Book of Lost Things* offers advice to the protagonist about routines: without purpose and an outcome, routines inevitably unravel into tedious, onerous tasks. If we are creating and directing the routines in our classroom, we might lose sight of what routines are valuable to our students and what routines are valuable to only us. For a routine to be effective, both student and teacher need to understand its purpose and value the outcome.

We invent or adopt many routines in our teaching careers. This book contains several examples from fellow educators. Like anything, though, some routines will work with some students, while other students will not respond. The concept of a routine in education cannot be fixed—it must be reconsidered when it no longer seems to be effective.

Routines Are Made to be Broken

"I never teach my pupils. I only provide them conditions in which they learn."
— Albert Einstein

We cannot go further in our exploration of routines without adding the following caveat: routines should not always be followed. Doing the same thing over and over with no change has long been connected with dazed eyes and robot-like voices—not the best image of engagement. Research in neuroscience has shown that making small shifts to daily routines can stimulate our brains and improve brain functioning. How does this apply to our classrooms? Be flexible on those days when the routines are disrupted. Purposefully change a routine once you notice it has become too automatic and comfortable. Have conversations around what positive things come when routines are broken. Philosopher Amos Bronson Alcott said, "The less routine, the more life." He likely never watched a class of thirty kids mob a pencil sharpener before a spelling test, but he does offer some sage advice about relishing (rather than dreading) those moments of unpredictability.

What Makes a Routine Effective?

When we consider where we need routines in the classroom, we typically look to tasks that are done on a regular basis and can easily be done independently.

Routines—also known as classroom procedures—rid students of distractions that waste time and interfere with learning. Guesswork is minimized. Minor frustrations and inconveniences are fewer, as are opportunities for misbehavior. The students, then, are left to focus on learning. (Linsin, 2009)

As with everything we do in our teaching practice, it is quickly obvious when a routine is ineffective because the classroom unravels like a poorly tied knot. I have many pencil stubs that were victims to a rather exuberant pencil-sharpening routine that went awry. Just as disastrous is creating a routine only to change it or forget it the following week. A useful guideline is that it generally takes thirty days to build a new habit, to make something automatic. Flexibility and change are essential to any classroom, but few people thrive in an environment that is in a constant state of unanticipated change. We need to create a classroom with consistency; then effective routines will provide the backbone of the learning environment.

We need to constantly reflect on keeping a routine effective:

- Does it have a clear purpose and outcome?
- Will the purpose and outcome be valuable to everyone?
- Can it be easily learned?
- Can anyone complete it?
- After a few weeks, is it automatic?
- Will we maintain it?

The Habit Loop

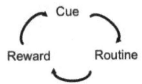

A simple neurological loop discovered by MIT researchers, the habit loop consists of three parts: the cue, the routine, and the reward. Charles Duhigg in *The Power of Habit* uses this loop as the framework for understanding our habits and he suggests ways to experiment with the habit loop to create healthier, more-positive habits. The habit loop is a powerful way of viewing routines we use in our classrooms and determining why they fail or flourish. In a classroom, the cue could be the morning bell, a messy desk, or a student's written draft; the routine follows this cue; and then there is some kind of reward (intrinsic or extrinsic). If the cue is unclear (for example, the morning bell is not loud enough for anyone to hear), the students will need prompting to start a routine around morning attendance. If the routine is unclear, the cue of a student's written draft will not prompt peers to edit the work and celebrate the learning. And lastly, if the reward is undefined, the desks will be perpetually messy and no one will bother keeping a clean and organized working space. All three parts are equally powerful and important. When a routine fails, the habit loop might offer insight into knowing what must change to create a productive habit.

Introducing Routines

Forming routines starts the moment we meet our students. It's the first step in the classroom—introducing pervasive routines. For instance, while we share our first class conversation, students are intently taking in information: our eye contact, our posture, if we allow interruptions, how much attention they are getting, and how to respond in the situation. The beginning of the school year is ultimately exhausting for teachers because, intentionally or not, we are constantly establishing routines.

Research on the management of students and establishment of rules shows, again and again, that a formal approach to teaching routines at the start of the year leads to a higher success rate in students (Cheney, 1989; Vallecorsa & deBettencourt, 2000). We all know that if we explicitly teach a routine to our students and the expectations are made clear, modelled, and practiced, then it has a better chance of lasting.

Traditionally, establishing classroom routines follows this process:

1. Teacher introduces routine
2. Teacher models routine
3. Students practice routine
4. Students master routine
5. Teacher expands on the routine

This approach works: students get it because this is what they expect. In this process, step 3 (students practicing the approach) is the most time-consuming. It was found that if teachers spend four days with a precise introduction, verbal description, and modelling, then the routine needs only to be cued by a single word or gesture after a thorough introduction (Leinhardt, Weidman & Hammond, 1987). In many situations, this process is the one to use. It works well for routines that leave little room for variety, such as how to use a pencil sharpener, where to find extra erasers, and how to hand in papers. Not everything can involve discussion and democracy, especially not actions that require a large degree of automaticity. That said, applying this process to all the classroom routines leaves little room for creativity or independent thought from our students, and it is not very motivating.

For routines that we hope will embed positive character choices in our students and that can be approached in more than one way, try this process:

1. Teacher or student introduces the problem
2. Students share routines to address the problem
3. Teacher and students discuss and collectively agree on a routine
4. Teacher and students model the routine
5. Teacher and students practice and master the routine
6. Teacher and students expand on the routine

Here, there is an additional step of discussing and agreeing on a routine; steps 2 and 3 are the most time-consuming. The big shift is that this process creates a different mood in the classroom. All of a sudden, student voices are valued, their opinions matter, and they feel integral to the class dynamic. The setting transforms from "my classroom" to "our classroom." The best part is that, once students feel they own the concept, they practice and master it quickly; they want to expand on it. They are intrinsically motivated because it is theirs. This approach is very effective for establishing a behavior management program, deciding on a problem-solving approach, determining where to store supplies and what to put on bulletin boards, etc.

In their research, Leinhardt, Weidman and Hammond (1987) noticed that if the teacher provides the script for the routine, the lesson moves quickly. However, they also noticed that when the students state the routine, their interest is maintained. Admittedly, a portion of teacher control is released in this process. But this is offset by a positive student response and more successful lessons or routines (Covino & Iwanicki, 1996).

The Transfer of Power

Imagine being asked to fill in this survey question: *Where do you put yourself on this continuum?*

Routine-Follower	Risk-Taker

Now consider this: *What if how we implement routines involves taking risks?*

Routines are an essential part of our day and are crucial to the classroom running effectively. But, as teachers, we do not need to be always holding the reins. Creating an environment in which our students feel valued and motivated to learn requires us to release the power. To make this transfer of power, we need to trust our students. Our students want to help; they want to feel special. Think of young students who want to be first in line, walk a note to the office, or hand out notebooks; consider how older students thrive when given responsibilities, such as the chance to visit another class to request a supply or fixing a computer problem. By passing the reins to our students, we are absolutely taking risks—healthy, necessary risks.

Each routine in this book is designed to empower and engage students. The routines are designed to push students to think, foster self-regulation, care, and collaborate. When searching for a routine to try, you will find within the format of the routines tools to identify routines to suit your needs. In addition to the steps required to set up the routine, each routine presented includes

- Title: helps identify its big idea
- Objective: a quick summary describing the routine's purpose
- Key Words: one or more attributes we hope to foster in students
- Suggested Grades: an age range that the routine might work best with:

    Early Primary: preschool and Kindergarten
    Primary: Grades 1–3
    Junior: Grades 4–6
    Middle: Grades 7–8

- Debrief: possible points for discussion after the routine; reflection on how the routines might work in your classroom

Objective, Key Words, and Suggested Grades for each activity appear in the margin, to help you quickly choose routines for your classroom practice.

Job Boards

Every classroom has many routines and tasks that need to be completed on a daily basis. And, frankly, teachers are needed in more important places than some of these tasks require. Think of parents dropping off their children, carrying their backpacks, making their lunches, cleaning out their lockers, and managing their social interactions. It is clear these children are a long way from independence. The same is true in the classroom. The more we do for our students, the less self-reliant they become and the more they depend on us for meaningless tasks.

So how do we break this helicopter approach? We let students do it. And we let them manage it without shadowing them and without bearing the consequences ourselves. The easiest way to implement student participation is to create a job board. Job boards can be introduced organically: two days into the school term, say, "I cannot handle X, Y, and Z. What can we do as a class to work together to get all of these tasks done?"; or you can brainstorm them with students the very first day of school. Regardless of when or how it is introduced, the collaborative creation of a job board immediately shares tasks, shows trust, and creates a classroom that works together. Regardless of how it is implemented, what you call it, or which roles are selected, the idea of students working as a team with the teacher to complete classroom tasks is vital.

When working together to create a list of necessary jobs, consider these:

- line leader
- door holder
- greeter to meet guests and manage telephone calls
- calendar helper
- weather person
- recess clothing monitor to ensure appropriate attire
- recess problem-solver to try to solve problems before involving the teacher
- days-of-school tracker
- snack distributor
- mail person/messenger to collect notes or hand out notes for the teacher
- desk surveillance to monitor cleanliness
- librarian to collect and return books
- substitute to take the role of teacher if you need to step out
- sweeper
- scheduler to post the daily schedule
- attendance-taker
- hander-outer of books/worksheets
- collector of work
- board-eraser
- recycling monitor to ensure trash and recycling go where they are intended
- supply distributor
- technician to attempt to repair electronic issues
- electrician to manage the lights
- homework checker
- gardener to keep the plants alive
- equipment manager

Managing the job board can also be implemented using a variety of strategies:

- Create one job per person and continually rotate the jobs
- Put two people on a job and have them work collaboratively to do it

- Rotate two groups in opposite directions, so each student works with a variety of others all year long
- Put half of the class on a job and half off, with students rotating each week
- Post non-jobs, such as "vacation," for a break in the cycle
- Post a class list and make one job the tracker of jobs, to ensure there is no doubling up on a job and that everything is managed fairly

The effectiveness of the student job board begins with teacher encouragement and reminders, and remains intact once students realize how easily the class flows when everyone does their job. It can lead to passionate class discussions when students fail to do their job or one student tries to take over and do the jobs of many—facilitating these complaints is a good introduction into any lesson in politics. Through the job board, other routines naturally flow forth to be adopted or suggested by students. Remember that the job board might require revisiting and revision at different points in the year, when you find jobs are not being done or not being valued. We have also found that about two months into the school year, tweaking is usually needed.

While the job board is a simple measure, it immediately sets the tone in the classroom—we are all responsible for our class community and each of us has a voice in what we value as a class.

This job board includes a list describing the jobs next to images of the jobs themselves.

CHAPTER 2

Beginning the School Day

The morning classroom is full of many things: the anticipation of students, the moods of everyone entering the room, and the promise of a new day. It is also where we help set the tone and navigate the day ahead.

Research shows that students and teachers are freshest in the morning. Taking time for morning routines helps our students

- develop confidence. They know what to expect and they feel ready and prepared.
- review previously taught concepts. Reviewing what was taught the previous day helps warm up students for a full day of learning.
- create a sense of comfort. They see the plan for the day and can anticipate what lies ahead.

We've all had those mornings—the coffee maker was broken, your own child forgot to tell you about a field-trip form, you didn't realize it was snowing outside—and arrived to our classrooms a bit scattered. Having morning routines established can help to ease our own transition into the school day, not only those of our students, as we enter the room and get organized for the day.

These routines were designed with student ownership in mind. The students can manage attendance, track the weather, and hand in notes, among many other things. Having these routines in place allows you invaluable time to connect with students, to discover how their evening was, to find out how are they feeling today, to touch base on a concept from last night's homework or today's class. Taking the time in the morning can set the tone for how the rest of the day unfolds (Freeman-Loftis, 2011).

Routines for Entering the Classroom

Entering the classroom can range from a mob of scrambling and pushing students to a militant marching order. These routines were created to enable students to individually determine how they would like to enter the classroom. They are created to release the task of organizing the entry to students, so that they trickle in at their own pace, prepared and organized for their day.

A Space for Each Student

Objective:
To ensure that students have their own space to organize themselves.
Key Words: independence, self-regulation
Suggested Grades: Early Primary/ Primary/Junior/Middle

As students arrive, they need to know exactly where they are going, what they need as they enter the classroom, and what they can leave behind.

- Create a space for each student. This could be a hook on the wall, a locker, or a cubbie.
- On the first day of school, explain the routine: where each student will put his/her belongings and how materials will be organized when they enter the classroom. If students have lockers, you might let them select their locker; include a conversation about choices and how the location of their locker is a personal choice.
- In a central location, post a clear anchor chart that lists how students will organize their spaces.
- When their spaces are established, have students personalize their spaces with a name tag or photos.

Choosing Lockers

Getting a locker is a rite of passage. As teachers, we often assign lockers without considering the factors that are important to students. Allowing students to select their own lockers, with guidance, makes the whole process of moving from cubby to locker more meaningful. Explain to students that the most influential factors are

- who is around that you can guide or that can guide you
- if you feel you have a strong sense of order and can be further away, or if you might need support and should select a locker closer to the classroom
- who is taller, who moves slower, and who will not mind waiting to get into their locker space

Once students have thought about these factors, they are free to select a locker; release them one by one. Students mark their lockers with sticky notes.

Debrief

By allowing students to select their own space, you are creating a relationship of trust, as well as holding them accountable for their choices.

Sorting Homework

Objective:
For students to organize themselves when entering.
Key Word: self-regulation
Suggested Grades: Primary/Junior/ Middle

- In a set spot, create a station for the students to organize their books and notes from home. It can be right by the door, or farther away to decrease crowding near the door.
- Bins or baskets can be labelled: e.g., Math Homework, Reading Journal, Notes from Parents, Agendas, etc.
- Students are responsible for sorting their homework and items from home as they arrive.

Debrief

Students can instantly see what they are missing. Homework, notes, and books are already separated, making it easier for you to find items and mark them.

Job: Mail Sorter

Objective:
To provide one student at a time with leadership and responsibility.
Key Words: self-regulation, student-driven
Suggested Grades: Primary/Junior

Assign the job of Mail Sorter to a student; assign on a rotating basis. Create an In bin and place it near the entrance. As students arrive, have them place all their belongings into the bin. The Mail Sorter sorts through the bin to create separate piles of work and notes; e.g., homework, reading folders, agendas. Using a class list, the Mail Sorter checks off students who are missing items

Debrief

- You can photocopy multiple class lists on one sheet and keep the checked-off lists with the handed-in work.
- If you have few items that come in each morning, this is an ideal job for one student. It helps students in organizing and provides them with responsibility.
- The Mail Sorter can issue passes to students who handed everything in neatly, or tickets to students who forgot an item.
- If you ask students to complete a morning task, consider exempting the Mail Sorter from the activity to complete the mail-sorting job.
- Having the Mail Sorter as a rotational job gives each student the chance to embrace this role.

Homework Notes

Objective:
To help students take responsibility of their incomplete work.
Key Words: self-regulation, assessment
Suggested Grades: Junior/Middle

- As students arrive, they follow the classroom routine and manage their homework.
- Place Homework Slips beside the bins. Use the templates on page 18.
- If students arrive without their homework, they need to fill out the slip and submit it to the teacher for record-keeping. It then goes back to the student for a parent signature.

Debrief

The slips inform parents that work has not been completed. They create an instant paper trail the student not only is aware of, but also created. This paper trail provides documented proof as a conversation-starter for a conference or when setting goals.

Morning Task

Objective:
To review previous work while students arrive.
Key Words: academic, independence
Suggested Grades: Primary/Junior/ Middle

- As students come into the classroom, have a set piece of work for them to complete.
- Tasks should be something the average student can complete in 10 minutes.
- All supplies for the task should be easily accessible. You might provide each student with a notebook or duotang for the morning task.
- Students can support and assist others when they have completed their own task.

Homework Slip

I, _____ , did not complete my

_____ homework as instructed.

It was due on _____ .

My homework is

☐ Incomplete

☐ Missing

☐ Not completed correctly as per instructions

☐ _____

My follow-up plan is to _____

Student Signature _____

Teacher Signature _____

Parent Signature _____

Homework Slip

I, _____ , did not complete my

_____ homework as instructed.

It was due on _____ .

My homework is

☐ Incomplete

☐ Missing

☐ Not completed correctly as per instructions

☐ _____

My follow-up plan is to _____

Student Signature _____

Teacher Signature _____

Parent Signature _____

Pembroke Publishers ©2015 *Classroom Routines for Real Learning* by Jennifer Harper and Kathryn O'Brien ISBN 978-1-55138-297-5

Debrief

Typically, the morning task is a follow-up activity to review a recently taught skill or concept. However, you can design the task to build on a concept students will be exploring later that day; i.e., using the morning task as a frontloading technique. The morning task can also act as a quick assessment of who can manage the task, if it needs reteaching, or if students are ready to move on to the next concept.

Headliners

- Using a variety of sources, such as newspapers, web articles, and radio, find two or three headlines from the daily news.
- Have a central area where students can record the headlines.
- As students enter the classroom, they can investigate the headlines and use a tally mark to indicate which headline they would like to discuss during a class meeting.

Objective:
Students use outside resources to research the headlines in the news.
Key Words: academic, critical thinking, curiosity
Suggested Grades: Junior/Middle

> These apps and websites are sources of age-appropriate news, along with the local newspaper and the website for national newspapers.
> Teaching Kids News: www.teachkidsnews.com
> Go Go News: www.gogonews.com
> Time For Kids: http://www.timeforkids.com/
> News-O-Matic: https://itunes.apple.com/ca/app/news-o-matic-daily-reading/id578023255?mt=8
> Smithsonian Tween Tribune (app and website): http://www.tweentribune.com/
> Scholastic News for Your Classroom: http://magazines.scholastic.com

Debrief

When structuring the school day, building in current events can be a challenge. Asking students to look for headlines encourages them to look into the current events. This activity fosters instant conversation and debate among students, as they discuss which headline needs to be a part of class discussion. For late arrivers, it can also become a critical thinking activity to guess the news story from the headlines. If possible, recording headlines in a more permanent way (e.g., chart paper, interactive whiteboard) makes them available for reflection later in the year.

Activity Action Cards

- Choose five independent activities that students can work on. These activities can be academic (e.g., multiplication flashcards, grammar games, cursive practice) and/or non-academic (e.g., board games, doodling).
- Once settled in the classroom, students select an action card from a small bin or an envelope hung on a board.
- Students independently engage in the activity until it is time for attendance.

Objective:
After entering, students are directed to an activity.
Key Words: academic, motivation, student-driven
Suggested Grades: Early Primary/Primary/Junior

Debrief

Action cards can be successful in getting students excited about the morning and the day. Students can suggest activities for the action cards, or activities can be based on key concepts the class is investigating at the time. To avoid some students playing board games every time, limit non-academic action cards and make clear that students must choose a different card every day of the week. Action cards can also be a handy tool if students need to be focused, separated, or practicing a task first thing in the morning.

Routines for Taking Attendance

Attendance, although mandatory, is not the most challenging task. These routines are created to empower students to take responsibility for recording their own arrival. Once relieved of the duty of calling names aloud, you are free to interact with students: shake their hands, ask important questions (e.g., "How was your sister's birthday party last night?"), or compliment anything you might notice (e.g., new haircut).

Graphing Attendance

Objective:
To build a class graph that requires each student to commit to a point of view.
Key Words: community-building, academic, critical thinking
Suggested Grades: Early Primary/ Primary/Junior/Middle

- Set up a graph on the chalkboard, whiteboard, or interactive whiteboard. It should offer students a choice or show a continuum.
- Place each student's name on a piece of cardstock or laminated paper for repeated use.
- Post a question on the graph. It could be
  - Something that builds on getting to know the class: e.g., *How many pets do you have?*
  - Something that builds on science skills: e.g., *What energy source do you feel is least disruptive to the environment?*
  - Something that builds on language skills or class reading: e.g., *What do you think will happen to Augustus Gloop?*
  - A chance to reveal emotions: e.g., *How do you feel about starting a new unit today?*
  - As students arrive, they place their name cards on the graph. The names that are not placed are the missing students.

Debrief

You can start with a simple T-chart and move toward more complex bar graphs, graphic organizers, and continuum lines as the year progresses.

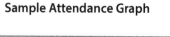

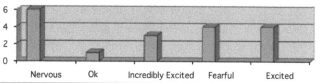

Sample Attendance Graph

I used this attendance graph to gauge the level of anxiety my Grade 1 students were feeling before their afternoon play performance. They submitted their results on a bar graph. Based on the results, I was able to navigate and respond to their emotional needs before the big show.

Reviewing Concepts

Objective:
To organize students quickly into work routines.
Key Words: academic, independence
Suggested Grades: Early Primary/ Primary/Junior/Middle

- Have a card with a task for each student in a visible spot.
- As students enter the room, they complete a morning task (see Morning Task on page 17) of reviewing the preceding day's work.
- Once the task is complete, have students put the work along with their cards into a bin.
- Early finishers check the board to see who is still working and ask if their classmates need support.
- Once everyone has completed the task, the remaining cards are absent students.

Debrief

This is an ideal method to review a concept prior to building on it. It is also a great way to organize materials for the day's lesson. For example, the card could read, *Place your story on your desk. Add a metaphor.* This sets up students for the writing lesson and encourages them to think about their story.

In a Kindergarten classroom, the task can be for students to identify their names on the board. As the year goes on, the students can start answering yes/no questions, such as *Do you like carrots?* by placing their names on the appropriate side of a simple chart.

Put Yourself on the Line

Objective:
Students make a judgment on a concept from the previous lesson.
Key Words: critical thinking, academic
Suggested Grades: Primary/Junior/ Middle

- Place a graphic organizer on the board.
- Have a card with each student's name on it.
- Make a statement that accesses their prior knowledge and that requires them to place a judgment on this information; for example, *The character of Templeton is mean* or *Perimeter is more useful than area.*
- Below the statement, draw a line. At one end, write *Strongly Agree*; at the other end write *Strongly Disagree*.
- As the students arrive, they read the statement, access their prior knowledge, and make a decision. Once each student has decided, he/she places his/her name card on the line in the spot that best represents the opinion they have.

Debrief

This activity easily leads into a rich class discussion in which students can support their opinions. If possible, allow students a chance to move their names on the line after the discussion. This will show active listening to others and gives them a chance to reevaluate their criteria.

Sample Opinion Line

What form of Government do you think is Lisa trying to form?

This example is from our unit on government. The students were reading "The Girl Who Owned a City" and this question not only prompted a lively debate, but also showed how much my students understood government and their novel study.

Extension

The line can be easily replaced with any type of graphic organizer, such as a Venn diagram or ranking ladder.

Throw a Ball Around

Objective:
To create a sense of community
Key Word: community-building
Suggested Grades: Early Primary/ Primary

- Use a ball or any other object that can be thrown around.
- Ensure that students know the names of their classmates in alphabetical order, or clearly post the names in order.
- Throw the ball to any student. The student with the ball reports the attendance of the first person in the classroom order by saying, "_____ is here" or

"_____ is not here." The student then passes the ball to someone else, who reports on the second person in the classroom order, and so on.

- Challenge the students to not throw the ball to the person who will be reported on next; i.e., no student should be reporting his/her own attendance.

Debrief

This activity builds an awareness of classmates and tracking who has the ball. It is also an excellent activity to reinforce a second language, as only two sentences are repeated.

Calendar Routines

Sharing what will happen during the school day builds excitement, calms anxiety, and helps students feel connected to class events. For each age group, the calendar routine will vary, but every classroom needs a clearly posted and understood plan for the day.

Morning Message

Objective:
Using a note for the class to share the day and set the tone.
Key Words: community-building, academic
Suggested Grades: Early Primary/ Primary/Junior

- Post a message that outlines details of the day or gives a hint of an activity. The message might review language patterns, slip in mistakes for students to catch, introduce new vocabulary, or have students identify sight words.
- Include a line that invites students to participate in the message: for example, *Draw a plant in our garden* or *Share a way to make 100*.
- As students arrive, greet them and invite them to read the message you have written for them.

Sample Morning Message

Message originally originally shared by teacher Gordon Scrunton on his blog http://gordonscruton.blogspot.ca

> Deer Students,
>
> Win you are righting something four my class, bee shore that you are using the write homophones. Eye cannot tale you enough how unintelligent you look win you use the wrong word. Their are know excuses four using the wrong words cause you have the education too no better. Your smart enough to no the differences butt you rush threw you're work and mess up.
>
> Sincerely,
> Ms. Harper

I used this Morning Message the day following a writing activity in which I noticed my students struggling with homophones. We used it to review homophones and emphasize the importance of using the right word. The word "cause" created quite a stir and prompted a subconversation about slang and word choice.

Debrief

The morning message is a great space to set up the students for the day, review concepts, or introduce a new skill. By making mistakes in our morning messages and having our students correct them, we are not only reviewing taught skills, but we are also showing students that everyone makes mistakes and that our classroom is a safe space to do so.

Track the Factors

This routine was shared by teacher David Orsorio.

- Keep track of the days of school in the form of a hundreds chart.
- Post a legend beside the hundreds chart with the numbers from 1 to 12.
- As a day is added, determine the math factors of that number. Use coding to mark factors on the chart: e.g., 3 is a blue x.
- Identify patterns and use the coding to predict the next numbers

Objective:
To keep track of the number of days in school, while embedding math skills.
Key Word: academic
Suggested Grades: Early Primary/ Primary

This photo displays the tracking system in action and how visual the patterns become. The number 60 was determined to be a "jumbo number" by students because it has so many factors. Mr. Orsorio helped students identify other jumbo numbers and compare their factors.

Debrief

In younger grades, there are often celebrations around the 100th day of school—an event that can be rich in math and literacy activities. This turns the days of school into a math game. The student can predict ahead to numbers with lots of factors. This reviews factors in an authentic and repetitive way, so that students quickly take ownership.

Visual Schedule

Objective:
Students put up the daily schedule and share it with the class.
Key Words: independence, self-regulation, community-builder
Suggested Grades: Early Primary/ Primary/Junior/Middle

- Write different subject areas on cue cards and attach a magnet to the back of each card. Keep a few blank ones handy for unanticipated changes.
- If applicable, have a classroom schedule posted nearby.
- Ask two students to post the schedule by arranging the cards on the board or whiteboard. Have them share it with the class.

> If you teach middle grades and students have a rotary schedule, e-mail them a digital timetable. Timetables can help students manage their time and get a sense of the day and week. In lower grades, the schedule should be visible all day.

Debrief

At the start of the year, have students write down the different activities/subject areas on cue cards and get them laminated. Many teaching blocks occur during consistent times, so students who are putting up the schedule are quick to pick out the cue cards for these regular lessons and to place them on the board. Students are proud to see their own work up each day as an important part of the classroom routines.

Weather Routines

Looking at the weather is one of those morning routines that seems unnecessary to students—until it affects recess. Mount a thermometer outside and you have an instant weather station. You can build on that with an empty pail as a rain collector and an easy spinning toy to determine wind. Or you can direct the students to the Weather Network or other online source of weather reports.

> *Tracking the weather not only reinforces science and math concepts, it can also lead into language lessons:*
>
> This morning [my students] and I were talking about the weather.... it was a fairly dismal conversation. We negotiated indoor recess, if it wasn't raining, just to be warm and cozy. I pulled up the Weather Network (as per our routine) and the icon on Toronto today was little specks and 4°. One boy commented, fairly loudly, "Oh, that is hell" (a bit of a shocking statement, but it represented the general feeling). Without missing a beat, another boy corrected him, "No, it is pronounced 'hail.'"

Graphing the Weather

Objective:
Students take a risk estimating the temperature.
Key Words: student-driven, academic
Suggested Grades: Early Primary/ Primary

- On the board or interactive whiteboard, post a simple pictograph with a range of possible temperatures along the bottom.
- When the first student arrives, explain that his/her role is to estimate the current temperature. Have the student write their name at, or drag it to, the place that indicates their temperature choice.
- As the rest of the students funnel in, have them consult with the first student for instructions.
- When all students have arrived and the graph is filled, bring the class together to discuss their estimations.

Debrief

This activity gauges the temperature for the day and helps students prepare appropriate recess attire. It can also review math skills: e.g., use prompts, such as *What is estimation compared to guessing? What clues did you use to arrive at your estimate?*; review data management skills and concepts, such as *majority, minority, mode, median, range.*

Do I Have to Wear a Coat?

Objective:
For students to determine appropriate outdoor attire.
Key Words: self-regulation, academic, critical thinking
Suggested Grades: Early Primary/ Primary

- Graph the weather each day for the first few weeks of school.
- Take students outside to experience what the temperature feels like. Discuss how it feels and what they would wear in that temperature.
- Once students are comfortable with assessing temperature, have them determine the temperature required for wearing a coat or jacket.
- Announce this temperature as the *No Coat Temperature.* Mark it on the thermometer or draw a line on a temperature graph.
- When students ask if they need a coat, refer them to the thermometer.

Debrief

If you use an electronic device or online source for weather, be sure to hide predictions, the afternoon high temperature, the "school day forecast." Leave it to students to determine if they need a coat. After all, what is the purpose of tracking the weather if we don't use the data?

Recess Clothing Monitor

Objective:
For one student to share information with classmates.
Key Words: critical thinking, academic
Suggested Grades: Early Primary/ Primary

- Assign one student the role of Recess Clothing Monitor.
- Place a visible reference for the student to determine the weather, or use the information from a morning conversation. Have the Recess Clothing Monitor post the items of clothing appropriate to the weather; e.g., light jacket, rain hat, mittens or gloves, sun hat.
- The Recess Clothing Monitor can also monitor for appropriate attire and issue follow-up notes or tickets.

Debrief

Quite often we share the weather during a morning discussion or circle time with younger students. Linking this discussion to appropriate recess attire helps make weather more relevant.

By assigning a student the role of Recess Clothing Monitor, we not only create a relevant discussion, but also bring accountability to our students.

CHAPTER 3

Building a Classroom Community

In 1916, John Dewey shared provocative statements about the need for an educational shift to "a fostering, a nurturing, a cultivating, process" (Dewey, 1916). And here we are a hundred years later, still agreeing. Our students grow academically, interpersonally, intrapersonally, and as a community. Our role as educators has always been to help nurture their minds and souls. Creating a strong classroom community is an essential part of fostering our students. Our classroom community is the foundation of our classroom. So what creates a caring classroom?

- **Belonging**: Students feel that they are part of the classroom, that people really know them.
- **Peer Connections**: Students feel safe in their relationships with their peers, and feel safe building friendly relationships.
- **Autonomy**: Students feel a sense of ownership and act on their inner beliefs, even when following routines, if they are provided with choice. Ironically, when we give students space to be creative and empowered by their choices, they come together as a team and community more strongly when it is required. It is the balance between group, individual, and whole-class activities that helps them thrive in each one.
- **Competence**: Students feel driven to learn, comfortable making mistakes, and capable of success.

"Striving to learn, to master one's environment, is a basic human characteristic." — S.H. Schwartz

The aspects of belonging, connecting, autonomy, and competence are interconnected.

When our students feel cared for by their teachers and peers, they are comfortable taking risks, making mistakes, and moving forward. They feel competent and are willing to be creative in their space. The routines in this chapter are all about creating a classroom in which our students feel safe, cared for, and connected. They are routines that we can establish to nurture a community, as well as to help each individual grow emotional intelligence.

Routines to Unify the Class

These routines are created to help bring the class together, to foster community spirit, to set up a learning and growing space, and to build a positive atmosphere.

What Stuck with Me

Objective:
To help students share information that is powerful to them.
Key Words: resilience, motivation, critical thinking
Suggested Grades: Early Primary/ Primary

This routine was shared by teacher Steph Donovan.

- Create a public space; i.e., a piece of chart paper, bulletin board.
- Each time a student finds something he/she finds profound, inspiring, or motivating, he/she writes it on a sticky note and posts it to share on this space.

Debrief

The public space you set aside becomes a powerful tool for students to share ideas and express what is meaningful to them or influencing them. On the interactive whiteboard, students can use a sticky-note tool. They can be inspired by their peers' posts of books, ideas, and perspectives.

High Fives

Objective:
To encourage students to recognize positive behavior in their peers.
Key Words: motivation, reflection, empathy
Suggested Grades: Early Primary/ Primary

This routine was adapted from Paul Faggion's Put-Up board, where students record positive put-ups for each other instead of negative put-downs.

- At the start of the year, begin modelling praise and high fives for students. Be explicit in your language: "Wow, Dylan, I want to give you a high five! You saw that I needed help with this math problem, and you came over to help me out."
- Keep High Five slips in a prominent spot in the classroom. When students want to give a High Five, they can write the details on a slip and give it to their peer. It can be anonymous.
- At the start of the year, you might give each student the name of another classmate to observe and give a High Five to. This helps establish that High Fives are not reserved for friends.
- Hang a name chart by the High Five slips so students can check off the name of the person receiving the recognition.

Debrief

When you start, this routine can seem a bit silly and the High Fives are often not very authentic; e.g., High Fiving a student who lends you an eraser. However, with time and consistent modelling, High Fives become rich observations about classmates.

> *I instruct students to focus on another peer once someone has received three High Fives from them.*

Team-Building Games

Objective:
To build community spirit.
Key Words: community-building, motivation
Suggested Grades: Early Primary/ Primary/Junior/Middle

Create challenging and fun tasks that need to be completed by the whole class. Some examples:

- Half the students make paper airplanes and then the entire class has to keep them in the air.

- Students form a circle and whisper a message along (Broken Telephone).
- Students form a circle, hold hands, and send a pulse (hand squeeze) around. Time students to see if they can beat their best time by working as a team.
- Each student makes a web from a piece of string and then has to get out of it.
- Students draw a picture together on a large piece of paper. You can use this as an attendance option, so participation is staggered.

Debrief

An occasional team-building activity goes a long way toward getting the wiggles out, refocusing students, and strengthening their relationship as a class. By making the goal to beat time or some other arbitrary concept, you have students working together to achieve the results, instead of competing with each other.

> In our Grade 1 classroom, Friday afternoon was Build It time. Students worked with partners, and partners and building materials were rotated each week. This gave each student a chance to work with everyone in the class at a few points throughout the year and to experience each type of building material. There are no objectives for Build It—it is free, creative time. However, an anchor chart was posted to define how to work together in partners.

Class Goals

Objective:
To work together as a class to set parameters for how the class should work.
Key Words: community-building, critical thinking, student-driven
Suggested Grades: Junior/Middle

This activity was created in collaboration with teacher Tina Jadgeo.

- Start with the big question, *What can we do to learn this year?*
- On the board, create three categories, for example:
  - Concrete Goals: goals that students can see happening; e.g., extra practice with a concept
  - Lofty Goals: goals that are a bigger step; e.g., teacher mentoring a student on a concept
  - BOGs, or Big Out-of-the-box Goals: goals that show the big idea; e.g., finding a new way to solve a problem or learn a concept
- Brainstorm goals to place in categories. You can also use concept attainment by having students come up with the category titles as you sort the goals.
- Work together to connect the goals and show how one leads to the other.
- Post the goals as an anchor chart and refer to it when a goal is achieved.

Students who brainstormed these class goals were passionate to monetize the achievement of a goal in Brain Bucks, and they quickly started brainstorming ways to fine/tax for improper use of their brains. This led into a nice discussion about making mistakes to learn.

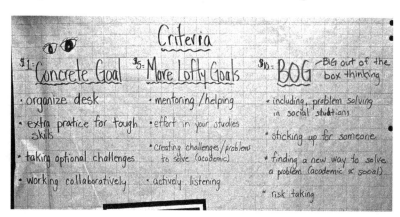

Debrief

To encourage goal-setting and follow-through, you can also link goals to a class reward system. Students can earn small, extrinsic rewards to build awareness of goal-setting and achievement.

Routines to Motivate the Class

Motivation is the desire or action toward a goal-directed behavior. In our classrooms, a student having the urge to do something shows a motivation.

- Extrinsic Motivation: the carrot on the stick; the urge to gain an external factor, such as a prize, bribery, or avoiding punishment.
- Intrinsic Motivation: a person's own desire; the urge to complete a task because it is important to them.

Our goal is to create intrinsic motivation in our students. We want them to achieve because they are driven to do so. However, we are also aware that we need to teach them how to set, work on, and achieve goals. When we develop a system, model it, and recognize goal achievement extrinsically, we motivate our students. It is an important step in creating self-driven students. Just as we teach them sentence structure to write stories, we teach them goal-setting and reward them to help them transition from external motivation to internal drive.

Class Rewards

Objective:
To create incentives for students to work as a team to attain a goal.
Key Words: community-building, motivation
Suggested Grades: Early Primary/ Primary/Junior/Middle

- At the start of the year, ask students what their favorite school activities are.
- As they brainstorm, give them parameters for the task. As these things will become incentives for the class, ensure that each activity can be managed within 20 minutes.
- Discuss how students can earn the chance to participate in these activities. Find a tool to track earned points toward these incentives (e.g., plastic toys, tokens). Students can earn points by doing various things in the classroom; e.g., lining up quietly, having no materials on their desks, asking an incredible question, getting a High Five from another teacher.
- Post the incentive list in a prominent place in your classroom. As the year progresses, remind students to add activities to the list.

Debrief

Discuss with students how many points are needed to earn an incentive activity. To maintain momentum, the number of points needed for each incentive should be low, and the ability to receive incentives should be frequent (weekly or bi-weekly).

Incentive Ideas

I make sure that incentives are not stickers or prizes; instead they are activities or special privileges. The whole class sharing the goal to earn an incentive motivates students to collaborate.

- Desk charms: random weird action figures that students can keep at their desks for a week

---

- 10 minutes of recess: a bonus add-on to the recess period
- YouTube screening: students submit appropriate clips for screening on the interactive whiteboard or computer projector.
- Select your desk partner for a day
- Eat lunch in the classroom with the teacher
- A class work period with music
- Auction tickets that can be used to purchase small prizes
- A picnic lunch outside
- Students can chew gum for one period.
- Night free from homework: parameters need to be in place; i.e., this pass applies to only routine work, like math sheets or reading
- 15 minutes of free time
- Sketchpad time or space to draw
- Access to special materials for indoor recess, such as paint or window markers
- Access to technology

From Extrinsic to Intrinsic

Objective:
To help students transition to intrinsic motivation.
Key Words: critical thinking, independence, motivation
Suggested Grades: Primary/Junior/ Middle

- Write goals for students on cards or pieces of paper: not individual goals, but goals that all students should be working on, such as, *hanging up our coats*. Post goals in public space.
- Create three categories for the goals: *Needs More Effort*, *Achieved By Most*, and *Intrinsic*.
- As part of the progression through the year, start to move goals from the first category to the second.
- Specifically teach intrinsic motivation. Explain that once we have mastered a goal, it gets moved to the *Intrinsic* category because we own it. It has become part of how we operate and we have grown because of it.
- Show that, as goals move to the *Intrinsic* category, then more, bigger goals enter the process in the *Needs More Effort* category. This a great platform to teach a growth mindset.

Growth Mindset

Researcher Carol Dweck explains that people can be placed on a continuum, based on where they think intelligence resides. People who believe that you are born smart or have innate abilities are considered to have a fixed mindset; they believe that you cannot change who you are. The term *growth mindset* applies to people who believe that success is a result of hard work. By teaching students a growth mindset, we empower them to learn; i.e., to make mistakes and to persevere. They understand that the process of learning is more important than the goal.

Debrief

The continuous movement of goals from extrinsic to intrinsic shows development in a big, visual way. To start the process successfully, create goals you know will be achieved in the first few weeks, such as hanging coats, putting lunch boxes away, or tidying up books. As part of the dialogue, make sure students understand the difference between equal and fair; i.e., putting away our lunches is an equal class goal but to be fair, and to help those who need it to succeed, we need to support our peers. Creating an anchor chart of *Words We Can Use to Help Our Friends* can help create a positive classroom atmosphere, in which students are working together to grow.

Routines to Consider Different Perspectives

Encouraging our students to consider different perspectives is a challenging task. It often begins with modelling as, during our class conversations, we share different ideas and points of view. Many teachers use literature as a base for opening up conversations about different perspectives. Building routines that encourage (and occasionally demand) students to think of a new perspective can help make class conversations richer and can nurture a more empathetic classroom, as we all understand that not everyone is going to agree with our point of view.

Breaking It Down

Objective:
Breaking down information into smaller steps or parts and considering each part separately.
Key Words: creativity, academic, critical thinking, empathy
Suggested Grades: Junior/Middle

- Share a story, event, or scenario.
- With your students, identify the key events. Use sticky notes or chart paper to record these key events.
- Use prompts to spark conversation as your class looks at each of the key events:
  - What choices were there?
  - If a different choice was made, would the outcome have changed?
  - Who or what inspired the direction of the events?
  - What other factors could have changed the events?
  - What do you think the author was intending when he/she wrote this part?
  - Whose perspective are you thinking from?
  - Do you have any questions from that perspective?

Debrief

Students often find considering different perspectives challenging because they do not have a grasp of all the information, or because a story might be too big to fully grasp in its entirety. By chunking the story, students can identify perspective from the smaller, and sometimes clearer, moments.

A Picture Is Worth a Thousand Perspectives

Objective:
To use works of art within the classroom to encourage conversations from different perspectives.
Key Words: creativity, critical thinking, empathy
Suggested Grades: Primary/Junior/Middle

- Collect a number of compelling artworks. You might begin with artworks that represent a certain time period or a historical event. These pieces are usually rich in detail and inspire many questions about the individuals portrayed in the works. You can introduce a piece of artwork at the start of a unit to inspire conversation or at the beginning of a creative writing lesson.
- Ask students to answer the same series of questions: *What do you see? What is happening here? What would it be like to be a part of this artwork?*
- Give students a chance to share their observations and ideas. Be impartial and remind the class that everyone might see something different when they look at a piece of art.

Debrief

Avoid sharing the story behind the artwork with students, as you do not want to train them to think they are guessing to find one right answer. Agree that every observation is a valid one.

> Artful Thinking is a program developed by Harvard Project Zero. Its aim is to encourage teachers to use artworks in their classroom to strengthen and inspire student listening and thinking. See http://www.pzartfulthinking.org/atp_palette.php for resources on how to use art within your regular teaching program.

More Than One Option

Objective:
For students to come up with different options for class problems or issues among peers.
Key Words: creativity, self-regulation, empathy
Suggested Grades: Primary/Junior/Middle

- Using the More Options graphic organizer on page 37, have students identify the problem and the steps that led to a situation becoming a problem.
- If the students are willing, have them fill out the organizer together. If they are still having a hard time seeing the different perspectives, they can each fill out an organizer to share with you and each other.
- After filling out the chart, have them share the situation from the other's perspective, if you feel they are emotionally ready to do so.

Debrief

I began using this method of problem-solving after dealing with irate students after recess. I realized that, for almost every problem, none of the "victims" or "culprits" consider any perspective other than their own. This method helps us have more caring conversations in class and it encourages students to be more active in solving their own problems.

Chart It Out

Objective:
To provide a space for students to voice concerns.
Key Words: self-regulation, critical thinking, reflection, empathy
Suggested Grades: Primary/Junior/Middle

- Provide students with a T chart of Pros and Cons; see sample.
- Provide space and time (e.g., during recess, after school) for students fill in the chart with their argument and then list the pros and the cons.

<table>
<tr><td colspan="2" align="center">**Sample Argument Chart**</td></tr>
<tr><td colspan="2">What I feel passionate about: _____</td></tr>
<tr><td>**Pros**
Show reasons why your argument is a good one.</td><td>**Cons**
How do other people feel about the issue? How could it negatively affect them?</td></tr>
<tr><td>

</td><td></td></tr>
</table>

Debrief

Often students have strong views and want to be heard. Providing them with space to think about their perspective and an opportunity to see another can create a more constructive conversation. They might need reflective quiet time to process what has happened.

Word Choice

Objective:
To help students understand the impact of their words and how they influence perspective.
Key Words: reflection, empathy
Suggested Grades: Junior/Middle

- Write and share a note or e-mail detailing a situation that models poor word choice. The word choice can be rude, demanding, offensive, or just presumptuous.
- Use the e-mail or note as a basis to discuss the impact of word choice on a reader: *What does this word choice tell you? What would the reaction be to this e-mail or note?*
- Together, brainstorm the important aspects of communicating: tone, word choice, details.

Debrief

In an era of digital technology, where our students struggle to realize their digital footprint and how the ability to send a message instantly affects others, taking time to teach tone and word choice is important. We need to explicitly teach perspective and how it affects others' feelings. We also need to show students how to communicate politely and appropriately.

> This e-mail prompted a conversation on approach and perspective:
>
> May I postpone my math homework (MJ pg 1–2) and study links to friday. Thanks, [student name]
>
> We discussed the etiquette of requesting information, and what the reaction of the teacher might be upon receiving this. We agreed that the letter should address the reader, provide detail as to why an assignment is not completed, and politely request a delay— without assuming it would be granted.

More Options

What's the situation?

_____

Use three words to describe how you feel right now

_____   _____   _____

Fill out the chart below and, if possible, think of alternative choices that would have helped the situation have a positive outcome.

What actually happened?	What were my other choices?
First…	I could have…
After that…	I could have…
Then…	I could have…
It ended…	If you chose the other choices, how would the situation have ended?

Share this sheet with your teacher and talk about your other options.

_____   _____
Signed   Date

Pembroke Publishers ©2015 *Classroom Routines for Real Learning* by Jennifer Harper and Kathryn O'Brien ISBN 978-1-55138-297-5

Routines for Celebrating the Individual

These routines are intended to endure through the school year—buzzing fresh in September and October, trudging through the dreary mid-year months, and pulling the class back into shape when the end is in sight. In a gentle, subtle way, these routines unite the class because they provide each student with what they need: recognition and celebration. And when we need it most, these routines direct our class back onto the positive track.

For celebrations of the individual, we need to ensure that all students are recognized. Keeping track on a class list goes a long way toward making sure no one is forgotten or that someone is not celebrated more frequently than others.

Understanding the Individual

- Have students reflect on themselves and how they act in various situations.
- Introduce the survey, explaining the various types of results.
- Have each student complete the survey or have them identify the traits on it they recognize as their own.
- Give students a moment to reflect on the results. Do they agree? Disagree?
- Talk about the strengths and how they might be used in situations?
- Use the traits as a springboard to talk about passions and learning.

> There are a variety of online surveys for students that will give them a sense of their strengths. We have always used the VIA Institute Character Survey because it accounts for cultural differences.
> http://www.viacharacter.org/www/

Debrief

There are many online tools and resources available to assess character traits. The trick is to really talk with students so that they understand they are not categorizing themselves or depicting themselves as one-dimensional. They need to understand that learning about their personality or learning styles can enhance their understanding of how they act in situations, how they respond to others, and how they learn. This is information that they will use to help them develop their passions and grow.

Filling the Emotional Bank

This routine was inspired by *Have You Filled Your Bucket Today: A Guide to Daily Happiness for Kids* by Carol McCloud.

- Have a short conversation with students about how the banking system works, with deposits and withdrawals.
- Create a space for each student's "bank" on a central bulletin board, beside each desk, or in class mailboxes.

- Print off Emotional Deposit Slips (see sample) and place them in a central location close to the buckets.
- Explain to students that when they share positive feedback in the classroom community they make others, and themselves, happy. By sharing kind thoughts and words, they are filling their Emotional Banks. When they feel down, they can remember all the deposits in their Emotional Bank, and make a withdrawal to feel better.
- Provide students with Emotional Deposit Slips. Ask them to fill out a slip for a peer. They need to give a positive anecdote about the peer or talk about a positive attribute they have noticed in the peer. Encourage them to be specific in their examples.
- Create a routine for reflecting on positive feedback after coming in from recess or before going home at the end of the day. Celebrate deposits in the Emotional Banks and encourage this activity by writing them yourself.

Sample Emotional Deposit Slip

Deposit Slip

To: _____

You _____

Sincerely, _____

Adapted from *Have You Filled Your Bucket Today: A Guide to Daily Happiness for Kids* by Carol McCloud

---

Debrief

Emotional Banks can be shared within and outside the classroom. They embrace academic skills, such as typing, writing, summarizing, editing. More importantly, they support and nurture the classroom community.

I was introduced to this idea by my son's Grade 1 teacher, Ms Shona. Although my son was a reluctant writer, he enthusiastically wrote notes for his peers. At home, he became more aware of the positive actions of his siblings and commented on them. During class meetings or parent nights, Ms Shona reminded parents to participate in filling the buckets, making us a part of the classroom community. Of all the Grade 1 materials, projects, and notebooks that came home in June, these are the only slips of paper we still read and dare not lose.

Go, You!

- In rotation, select a student a week.
- The class brainstorms positive words to describe the student, justifying the description with an action that they have witnessed: e.g., Julien is *caring* because he helped Patrick when he was hurt at recess.
- The list of positive words and actions are recorded and sent home with the student.

Objective:
To come together as a community to celebrate an individual student.
Key Words: community-building, reflection, motivation
Suggested Grades: Early Primary/ Primary/Junior/Middle

Debrief

Celebrating each student is important; coming together as a class to celebrate a student helps each child feel like an important part of the community. However, it is the justifying of the words that is the behavior changer. As the year progresses, students become more aware of their actions and how they affect others positively. These positive actions will become more frequent in their interactions and play. Older students can e-mail you a few words to explain why the student is being celebrated. These words can be fashioned into a word cloud to create a powerful image for the student.

Weekly Badge

Objective:
To reinforce necessary behavior in your classroom community.
Key Words: community-building, reflection, motivation
Suggested Grades: Early Primary/ Primary

- Assess the classroom and pinpoint two or three important behaviors that need reinforcing; e.g., active listening, transitioning, organizing materials.
- Create a badge to symbolize each of these traits; e.g., *Most Improved Active Listener*.
- At the beginning of the week, gather students and share who earned a badge the preceding week. Debrief with the class what the individual did to earn the badge. That student can proudly wear the badge or keep it on his/her desk for the week.

Debrief

Positive reinforcement is vital to any classroom and for all students. However, it is useless if falsely earned. If no one has earned a badge, then no one should get it. But if you witness and want to encourage an unexpected behavior, you can create a badge for it, define it for students, and celebrate it. By being flexible about the traits you support, you create a space in which students can help define what makes a positive impact. This will encourage more positive behavior, allowing students to be creative about how they contribute to the classroom community.

Objective:
To reinforce positive behavior by quietly celebrating individual actions.
Key Words: community-building, reflection, motivation
Suggested Grades: Early Primary/ Primary/Junior/Middle

Leave a Note

- Observe your students, looking for positive behavior.
- At the end of the day, or the beginning of the next day, leave a note for a student, describing his/her positive action. The note can be a sticky note on

the student's desk, written in the student's agenda (so they can celebrate with their parents), or a brightly decorated piece of paper on the student's desk.
- Keep track of who you are writing notes to and how frequently, as this can act as valuable modelling of fairness.
- As the year progresses, open up this activity to all students and encourage them to send their own notes to each other.

This note was written to a reluctant reader who took the risk of sharing his favorite book during a class book-share. It was a real turning point for the student, who had never completed a chapter book.

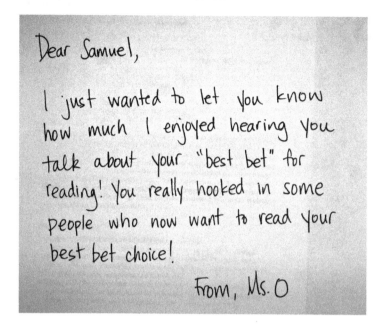

Dear Samuel,

I just wanted to let you know how much I enjoyed hearing you talk about your "best bet" for reading! You really hooked in some people who now want to read your best bet choice!

From, Ms. O

Debrief

I am constantly surprised at how effective positive reinforcement is. These little notes go a long way toward encouraging positive behavior and building rapport between you and your students.

Name Spelling Bee

Objective:
That all students in the class learn one another's names and the spelling of one another's names.
Key Words: independence, community-building
Suggested Grades: Primary/Junior

- Close to the start of the year, give each student a class list. Include one or two student names in each weekly spelling list.
- With younger children, use first names only. Encourage older students to learn last names as well.
- I usually don't ask the students to memorize last names, but to know them by sight.

Debrief

This activity is very simple but effective, especially for students whose names are not very familiar or easy to spell. Being able to spell a peer's name is a small but powerful way to build respect and community in a classroom. It has many extensions, too; e.g., graphing two-syllable names in the class, organizing names alphabetically.

Tweet It!

Objective:
To give students a chance to share something about themselves or their work with the class.
Key Words: critical thinking, motivation
Suggested Grades: Junior/Middle

- At points during the school week, ask students to "Tweet" aloud.
- Remind them that they only have 140 characters; get them thinking about approximately how many words that is.
- Give students a topic: e.g., *How did you feel about the activity we just did?* or *What did you do this weekend?* or *Who is your hero and why?*
- Give students a few moments to think about the topic, before saying their Tweet aloud.

Debrief

This activity became very popular in my Grade 4 classroom, with some students counting the characters. It helps students to think about their class contributions more critically and to focus their ideas on essential information.

Routines for Refocusing

John Medina, a developmental molecular biologist, researched how the brain works and how to learn effectively (Medina, 2008). When he discovered that the brain loses focus after ten minutes, he designed his 50-minute lectures around ten-minute intervals. Each interval explored one main concept and was finished with a "hook," an emotional trigger that related to the topic and showed closure. If our brains lose focus after ten minutes, how can we possibly sustain our students' attention for longer? These routines are tricks that help young brains refocus so that they can succeed.

Calming Down

Objective:
A consistent routine for calming down.
Key Words: self-regulation, independence
Suggested Grades: Early Primary/Primary/Junior

- Create a Calm Down anchor chart, with visuals for younger students, and post it in a calming area.
- The calming area can be a separate part of the room, or the anchor chart can be integrated into a whole-class routine after recess or an intensely busy period.

Sample Calm Down Anchor Chart

- Take several deep breaths
- Count backward from 10 slowly
- Use self talk: "I am calming down," or "I can do it."
- Think calm thoughts

Debrief

This routine can be modelled to the whole class, especially after recess or a busy period. Once implemented, it can help individuals who need to self-calm.

Gentle Reminders

Objective:
To create a subtle and caring system to limit distractions.
Key Words: reflection, self-regulation
Suggested Grades: Early Primary/Primary/Junior/Middle

- Spot a student who is beginning to distract others or needs a reminder to refocus.
- Take an indirect route to that student's desk, so that others do not get further distracted.
- Offer a small physical strategy to refocus the student: e.g., a tap on the desk, a gentle touch on the shoulder, putting the pencil down on the sheet of paper.

Debrief

Refocusing a student in a non-confrontational manner helps him/her save face with peers and keeps the distraction to a minimum. If you respect students' emotional needs, they respect you and are keen to get back on task.

> Teacher Elaine Rowlands uses a hand signal, putting up a finger for each distraction. Her students know that when she gets to three, they will have a conversation about their behavior. This helps students track their choices and it also makes them aware of the impact they are having on others.

Brain Break

Objective:
To provide a mental break when students are engaged in activity that requires long, sustained focus.
Key Words: motivation, community-building
Suggested Grades: Early Primary/Primary/Junior

- Assess the needs of the class; are there some students who have been sitting or focusing for too long? Are pencils being sharpened when they are already sharp? Are many students asking for a water break? Does everyone need a chance to refocus?
- Call students to their feet. If you use a consistent phrase, such as "Brain Break," then students will become accustomed to the routine of starting and stopping.
- Play a repeat-after-me game in which students copy your movements and sounds. Make the movements and sounds progressively more challenging.
- Shake it off and send students back to task.

Debrief

Some assigned tasks are just too long. Brain breaks are essential and effective when having young children complete a longer task. They enjoy the break, giggling while copying silly actions. Once this activity becomes routine, students who struggle with focusing will begin to come to you and request Brain Breaks, demonstrating self-regulation of their needs.

> John Ratey, the author of *SPARK: The Revolutionary new Science of Exercise and the Brain*, suggests that even a few minutes of exercise a day can offer physical and mental health benefits. A routine that encourages active movement is a simple way to get students moving and help them refocus their attention and energy.

Coping Toolbox

Objective:
To provide students with a set of coping tools to calm down or refocus after a stressful moment.
Key Words: self-regulation, independence
Suggested Grades: Early Primary/Primary/Junior

- Brainstorm with students items that help them calm down, based on sensory needs:
    feel (soft, smooth)
    smell (candles, lotions)
    see (snowglobes, happy pictures)
    hear (rainsticks, music)
- As a class, fill a box with de-stressors and place it in a quiet space or close to the door.
- Explain to students that these are intended for stressful moments, when they need help calming down.

Debrief

As much as these items will help students feel comforted when they need to de-stress, you also need to ensure they do not become just toys in the classroom. Placement of the box will determine if it becomes forgotten or overused, or if you find the balance to meet students' needs.

Routines for Transition Time

Our days are filled with transitions, as we change from math to language or from guided reading to inquiry. These transitions require the movement of many bodies and materials. They are also times when we lose our students and have to use "teacher voices" to gain back control. These routines keep the flow through transitions smooth and calm.

Musical Interlude

Objective:
To use music to transition from one subject to another.
Key Words: self-regulation, independence
Suggested Grades: Early Primary/Primary/Junior

This routine was shared by teacher Guillaume Dupre.

- Prepare by outlining the expectations for the next subject in a consistent manner and space, so students know where to look for this information.
- When it is time to transition to the next subject, play a song that sets that mood.
- Ensure that the song is long enough to allow students to put away current materials and prepare for the next class.

Debrief

Music has that wonderful way of shifting the feeling in the classroom. It sets a mood and students instantly recognize that the atmosphere has changed. If you allow students to create a class list of songs and use some of their choices, you empower them and make transition time a bit more flexible, while still maintaining the same routine.

Objective:
To smoothly transition from one
   subject to another.
Key Words: self-regulation,
   independence
Suggested Grades: Early Primary/
   Primary/Junior/Middle

Eyes on Me, One–Two–Three

This routine was shared by teacher Elaine Rowlands.

- Get the attention of students; see box for ideas.
- Popping up one finger at a time, show three fingers, each representing one instruction.
- Let students know how long they have to complete the transition.

Ideas for Attention-Getters

- Sing the first part of a song or phrase and have the students finish it.
- Use a noisemaker or a musical instrument.
- Flick the lights off and on.
- Post a visual timer (see Countdown Timer on page 64).
- Call out, "Voices!" in a loud voice; have students reply with "Sssh"; continue calling out "Voices" with your voice getting quieter each time and with students copying your tone and volume.
- Call out, "Rock!" and have students freeze as they say, "Star" back to you; let them freeze like rock stars! Change it up by letting them freeze like Mona Lisa (quietly, with hands on lap), Harry Potter (poised with wand in hand), Wayne Gretzky (taking a shot on net), or other well-known characters.
- Create a pattern of hand claps and have students repeat it.
- Bring your voice to a whisper until everyone is listening.
- Have students create a hand signal when you say a specific word.
- Provide a series of movement instructions, waiting until all are participating.

Debrief

Calling the class to attention and providing instruction is a timeless teaching strategy. However, restricting the instruction to three key points and providing them with an outlined time to complete them complements current brain research. We are not overloading our students with too many steps or rushing them to do it right away.

Routines for Solving Problems

When I think about problem-solving routines, I picture a traffic light with red to stop, yellow to slow down, and green to go ahead. My only problem is that I live in a major city, where most cars race through the yellow light in an attempt to not stop. This is the behavior that adults model. In the classroom, students race away to avoid stopping. They are not dealing with the problem.

There are two ways to deal with problems: proactively and reactively. The routines on shifting perspective and building a classroom community attempt to unify the class and proactively solve problems. That said, we are all human and emotions are always going to get into the way of a good routine. So how do we deal with problems reactively? What routines can we establish?

Solve the Feeling

Objective:
For students to reflect on a situation and identify the other person's concern.
Key Words: reflection, empathy, creativity
Suggested Grades: Early Primary/Primary/Junior/Middle

- Have students with a conflict share their stories, one after the other.
- When both have shared their own stories, it is their job to think about the other person's story and identify the main emotion that person may be feeling.
- Students need to work backward and help find a way to solve the concern and the emotion—not the issue.

Debrief

By taking away the highest moment of conflict and focusing on emotions, students develop their empathy.

Break a Glass

Objective:
For students to move beyond saying "I'm sorry" to solving the problem.
Key Words: community-building, empathy
Suggested Grades: Early Primary/Primary/Junior/Middle

- In front of the whole class, break a glass object to create a dramatic effect.
- Approach the broken object and say, "I'm sorry."
- Give a moment for students to process what you have done.
- Discuss with students:
  What just happened?
  Did I solve the problem?
  Is the glass fixed?
  What does the glass represent?
  Is "I'm sorry" enough? Does it solve the problem?
  What can be done to solve problems that affect people's feelings?

Debrief

Keeping the broken glass in a visible space reminds students that feelings are important and can be fragile. Referring to the broken glass during conflict-resolution discussions makes this an ongoing routine.

Pathways

Objective:
To help students find alternative solutions to problems.
Key Words: creativity, community-building, reflection
Suggested Grades: Primary/Junior/Middle

- Using an interactive whiteboard or chart paper, write a common group or class problem in the centre.
- Around the problem, create brainstorm spokes; call them *pathways*.
- Challenge students to think of ways to solve the problem, both appropriate and inappropriate. The only caveat is that the suggestions must be realistic.
- After spending a few minutes gathering possible solutions, go through the brainstorm and sort out the ones that would negatively affect others or oneself.
- Circle the solutions that could be viable and discuss what actions would be needed to make these solutions realistic.
- Remind students that next time they encounter the problem, they need to visualize these solutions.

Debrief

We all get in a solution rut, but taking time to look at alternatives reminds everyone that we can solve problems differently. It empowers students to look at recurring problems through a different lens or viewpoint.

Recess politics can be a hotbed of arguments. This photo shows problems a student identified around the game Four Square, as well as solutions for each. The student presented this pathway brainstorm to the class.

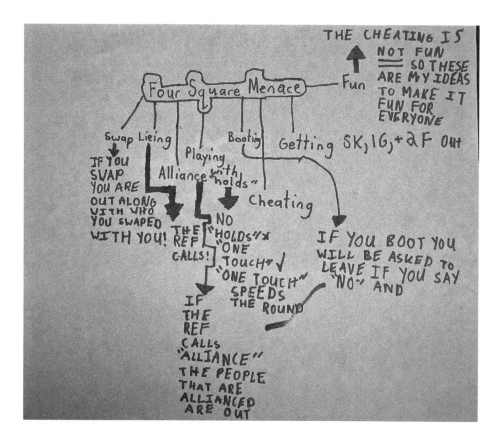

Your Problem Has a Solution

Objective:
To encourage students to consider solutions to their problems.
Key Words: creativity, reflection
Suggested Grades: Primary/Junior/ Middle

- This routine is very simple. If a student comes to you with a problem, he/she must be able to provide a reasonable solution for his/her concerns.
- At the start of the year, encourage whole-class discussions around common problems and possible solutions.

Debrief

American author Norman Peale said that within every problem are seeds to its solution. Let students know that you are open to hearing about their problems, but they need to come up with a solution as well. It helps build responsibility, as students often realize that part of the solution is changing their own behaviors.

Solution and Resolution

Objective:
To empower students to resolve a problem.
Key Words: accountability, student-driven
Suggested Grades: Early Primary/ Primary/Junior/Middle

- After a mildly chaotic event, bring students together.
- Explain the problem and ask them how they could resolve it. Brainstorm ideas.
- Step away and leave the problem for students to solve.

Debrief

Quite often we want to follow a checklist on how to solve problems and offer solutions. But some problems are not so easily solved. By creating the space for students to find their own solution, we also help them find closure.

In our classroom, an unidentified student experimented with a crayon in the only electric pencil sharpener. I had fixed the sharpener many, many times, but this time I looked to my class in defeat. I brought out a small handheld sharpener and offered it to them. This prompted a series of "heroes" to come to the electric sharpener to fix the problem. Days passed and many gave up. But one, a little boy who is easily distracted and always off task, stuck to the problem and fixed the sharpener. When I recognized the moment, he claimed it and shined.

CHAPTER 4

Independent Work and Executive Functioning

Establishing routines around independent work has a definitive goal in mind—creating an independent student. As we create and use routines, we need to ask ourselves if the routines will eventually encourage independence; for example, setting routines to manage supplies so that students do not need to ask the teacher. Once I witnessed a complicated routine of putting away materials that involved the teacher giving signals for each material and students bringing the bins to the teacher to be put away. All the students participated, all the bins were put away neatly, and everything was accomplished in less than five minutes. But without the teacher or another adult to direct the task and give the signal, the students could not put away their materials. It was a routine that cultivated dependence, not independence.

Executive functioning is a term for the mental processes that help us self-regulate and self-direct. In a classroom, the academic skills associated with executive functioning—e.g., paying attention to detail, remembering things, planning, organizing and strategizing how to complete tasks—are instrumental to a student's ability to work independently. Having clear and consistent routines in the classroom to support and promote independent work habits provides strategies to help with executive functioning challenges.

Mini-Routines to Support Executive Functioning Challenges

- When assigning a task, break it into chunks and provide time guidelines for each section.
- If using an agenda, assign time limits for the various homework tasks.
- Have a visual schedule in a prominent space in the classroom; refer to this schedule with each transition.
- Have visual reminders of daily tasks or activities; e.g., a poster that describes how to get ready for the day.
- When creating a description of a task, make a checklist: break the task into steps and add a blank check box beside each step.
- Have a consistent routine to signal transition times.
- Schedule a weekly cleaning out of desks or bins.
- Provide designated spots for handing in work.
- Have a consistent cue to remind students to turn in work.

The eventual goal of sharing and establishing routines in our classrooms is to foster an intrinsic ability to manage oneself. We aim for that delicate balance between developing executive functioning techniques and building intrinsic motivation, so that students embrace self-management routines. These are the building blocks for a solid foundation of learning.

Routines for Managing Supplies

Enabling our learners means providing them with the tools they need to complete their tasks. They need to feel empowered to find and use supplies when they need them. That said, watching an exuberant Kindergartener with a glue stick is a good reminder that encouraging independence around managing supplies is not the same as free reign. We want our students to have strategies to manage their needs within a class, while also developing respect for the classroom supplies that need to last through a school year and beyond. These routines are created in the attempt to find that balance.

Labelling

Objective:
For students to feel ownership of the room by labelling the bins.
Key Words: community-building, student-driven, curiosity
Suggested Grades: Early Primary/ Primary/Junior/Middle

- Stop yourself from labelling key items in your classroom in preparation for the new school year.
- Explain to students that the room needs to have clear labels so that everyone will know where everything is.
- Give students a chance to wander, explore, and locate items.
- Provide each student with a marker and labels or sticky notes.
- Have students working alone, in pairs, or in groups label bins and spaces in the classroom.

Debrief

The beauty of students labelling the classroom is twofold:

1. You do not spend countless hours creating pretty, but arbitrary, labels you hope students will read.
2. Students feel that they own the classroom. They can direct each other to the supplies, because they labelled them.

> In my Grade 1 classroom, I encouraged inventive spelling, and this means that the classroom labels did not use accurate spelling. As the year progressed and we learned new spelling patterns, we would revisit the labels and see if any of them needed to be replaced. By midyear, the spelling of all labels was correct and the students had taken ownership over the supplies.

Classroom Scavenger Hunt

Objective:
For students to get a sense of where supplies are in the classroom.
Key Words: community-building, student-driven
Suggested Grades: Early Primary/Primary/Junior/Middle

- At the start of the year, draw a map for the classroom. Include only the furniture that will not be moving, along with a few reference points.
- On the first day of school, ask students to mark on the map the important items that they will need throughout the year.
- Post the map in an accessible place.
- As the year progresses, return to the map and ask students to find relevant items on it; e.g., protractors when beginning a geometry unit.
- When you introduce new items, add them to the class map.

Debrief

Having ownership of the map allows students to determine what the important items in the classroom are. This is a wonderful tool to share with supply teachers, as it lists where they can find everything they might need.

Science Proves It

Objective:
Proving to students the value of properly managing consumable supplies.
Key Words: academic, self-regulation, curiosity
Suggested Grades: Early Primary/Primary/Junior

- Set aside a small part of the room or a table as the Science Experiment Area.
- Ask students what school supplies do not last long.
- Bring one of the items into the science area and perform the Careless test to show what happens when the item is left without proper care: e.g., leave a marker's cap off, or a glue bottle not sealed properly.
- Track what happens when the item is not cared for.

Debrief

Follow up this activity by exploring how the items are made for a fun way to start the year. The sacrifice of one marker and glue stick in September saves the lives of many more throughout the year. Although this seems to be a one-off activity, students can always return to the Science Experiment Area to find more efficient uses for paper, or any science inquiries they might have. This is a good opportunity to cover science concepts. For example, in the case of glue and markers, the word *evaporation* could be linked to students' observations.

There are two rules for our "maker table" or science space where the students are free to explore and build on their learning hands-on: it is collaborative, so anyone can build on anyone else's design; and it does not get cleaned up. It is the students' favorite part of the classroom.

Back Where It Came From

Objective:
Getting students to help put away materials.
Key Words: self-regulation, student-driven, community-building
Suggested Grades: Early Primary/Primary/Junior/Middle

- In order for this routine to be effective, supplies need to have a regular spot within the classroom that is known to students.
- Prior to taking out materials, briefly talk to students about how the materials are organized. If materials come from a work space or centre area, consider taking a photograph of how it looks when it is clean to hang by the area so students have a model to guide them.
- Decide on a reasonable time limit for putting away the materials. Use a timing device that is clearly visible to all students.
- For larger jobs, create clean-up cards to give to students for the tasks that must be completed.
- Inspectors (you or designated students) can check the classroom after the clean-up is done. Keep expectations high—that each marker (with lid intact) will find its way home to the correct bin.
- As an incentive, I give a class reward for getting an area clean within a given time limit.

Debrief

During really great teaching moments, we've got everything out—markers, glue, sticky notes, chart paper—whatever it takes to create and cultivate the learning experience. So having a clear routine around clean-up is essential. No matter the age level, set your sights high and make sure you have enough time for clean-up. It is a simple routine, but it works.

Simple Storage Tips

Organizing classroom supplies so that they are accessible and manageable is a bit of an art form. These tips and tricks are low-cost suggestions for maximizing the organization of your classroom and to encourage low-maintenance routines around classroom supplies.

- Classroom supplies should be visible and accessible.
- Prioritize supplies that you use most and give them the most prominent place in your classroom.
- Put supplies close to where you want them used; for example, store clipboards in the reading area where students do independent work on the carpet and need a hard surface.
- Use one bulletin board as a hanging area for essential folders: e.g., supply information, emergency contacts, etc.
- Organize supplies by subject.
- Bigger is often better; avoid storage containers with many small fiddly spots. Individual desk or table containers work well for a few weeks, but are hard to maintain.
- Consider storing drawing utensils by color.
- Resealable bags are an essential tool. You can fill them with smaller items (like reinforcements or erasers) and hang them from the board or bulletin board.
- When possible, get clear bins so students can see what is inside.
- Avoid cute names or unusual fonts and patterns. Make labels clear and logical. Instead of the "Whoops I made a mistake!" Bin, just call it an eraser bin.

Paper Sticks

Objective:
To encourage reuse of supplies.
Key Words: community-building,
    motivation, empathy
Suggested Grades: Junior/Middle

- Set parameters for what qualifies as scrap paper; e.g., a piece of paper that is larger than your hand, with no ripped corners. Have a scrap-paper bin visibly available in the classroom near your regular paper supplies.
- Close to the paper supplies, have a container with craft sticks, with each stick representing one fresh, unused piece of paper. When a student uses a piece of new paper, they must take a stick. If a student uses a piece of scrap paper, they do not need to take a stick.
- Once students have depleted the craft sticks, they need to complete a green action to trade their paper sticks for a piece of paper.

Debrief

Paper sticks succeed when students understand why they are using them. Show a quick video or discuss the impact of the ecological footprint to transfer this routine into empathy for the environment.

I started this system after watching my students create their own information boards; the waste of paper was incredible, with little thought for using scrap paper. When I introduced the paper sticks, students became very creative with how they used the paper resources in the class. Green actions the students brainstormed included litterless lunches for a week, a day without lights in the classroom, planting a plant at home or at school, walking somewhere for an errand instead of driving, and telling someone to turn off their car instead of letting it idle.

In Bin

Objective:
Collecting student work.
Key Words: self-regulation,
    independence
Suggested Grades: Early Primary/
    Primary/Junior/Middle

- Have an area designated in the classroom where all work to be assessed is handed in. Label it the *In Bin*.
- Post by the In Bin a reminder about what completed work looks like.
- Have a student sort the work in the In Bin and check off who has completed what tasks.
- Clip completed work together for assessment.

At the start of the year, I create a document with four or five columns, each containing a class list. I cut these columns apart and have a whole bunch of class lists ready to use. I even laminate a few, so I can reuse the lists throughout the year.

Debrief

The In Bin can be a life-saver. Loose papers deposited on my desk are easily lost, and having one central spot where students hand in work has helped me monitor what work has been handed in through a quick visual scan. It also helps prevent "I handed that to you, Teacher, but you must have lost it" conversations. If it is in the In Bin, it is IN. If not, it is out!

Routines for Technology Management

Unlike pencils and duotangs, laptops and tablets are expensive tools. In order to ensure your school or class computers are optimally used, you need to have routines around correctly storing these materials and managing their use within the classroom.

Things to consider when developing routines around digital technologies in a classroom:

- Assigning a student or team of students to be the tech crew, whose job is to check that all the devices are properly plugged in.
- What cues you need to give students when they are working on digital devices. A clear signal, such as "Laptop lids down" or "Tablets face-down," can help remind students to focus when listening to instructions.
- Creating a digital time check as a class or as part of your personal planning, calculating how much screen time you include in a teaching day. The current school of thought among Canadian and American doctors is that children under the age of 12 should not have more than two hours of screen time per day; this includes time spent using TV, computers, cell phones, video games, and movies.
- Having clear guidelines around how to travel from place to place with a laptop or tablet.
- Providing a sense of ownership by assigning individuals to certain shared computers. This will help establish a sense of responsibility.

Organized Device Storage

Objective:
For students to be responsible for maintaining class or school devices.
Key Words: independence, self-regulation
Suggested Grades: Early Primary/Primary/Junior/Middle

- Label each classroom device with a number.
- Match this number to a specific spot in the storage system.
- Teach students how to store, charge, and remove the devices from storage.

Debrief

If there is a set spot for each device, the chaos is limited when the activity is over and all the devices need to be returned to their spots. A number system allows you to call in "odd numbers" or "prime numbers," or "numbers that are divisible by 2": this limits the number of students accessing the storage at one time and can act as a quick math review. The final benefit to a labelled system is quick identification if a device is missing and quick tracking to find who is responsible for it.

Building Small

Objective:
To slowly introduce the use of technology in the classroom.
Key Word: self-regulation
Suggested Grades: Early Primary/Primary/Junior/Middle

- Ensure that classroom routines and expectations are being met without the use of technology.
- Begin by replacing one routine, centre, or activity with technology; for example, building words with block letters is replaced by building words on the interactive whiteboard.
- Once students show success at one activity, add more to suit your comfort level.

Debrief

By starting small and substituting one activity at a time, students gain a structured awareness of what expectations are. They also have a chance to practice their collaborative skills prior to the introduction of technology, allowing for a smoother transition. This routine helps build confidence in teachers who want to slowly build their technology comfort level.

Technology Agreements

Objective:
To build a bank of agreements that students will follow when using technology.
Key Words: self-regulation, reflection
Suggested Grades: Early Primary/ Primary/Junior/Middle

- Prior to the first power button being pressed, have students make a list of rules they agree to follow when using a technology tool.
- Post the list and have the students sign it.
- As the year progresses, return to the list to ensure that everyone is still acting responsibly.
- Add and modify the list as students prove to be more responsible.

Debrief

By agreeing on a list of rules, the class is instantly accountable. As the year progresses, lists of rules will need to expand and cover topics not apparent at the beginning of the year; therefore, a posted list is ideal, as it can be modified, adjusted, and expanded. Transferring these agreements to a chart makes for an easy checklist to see who is being responsible for their technology.

For Real

Objective:
To provide students with a routine to ensure the validity of websites.
Key Words: critical thought, independence
Suggested Grades: Junior/Middle

- After a lesson on Internet literacy, create a class list of questions to evaluate online resources.
- The list can be made into a checklist and stapled to a student's jot notes from online resources. Or the checklist can be in poster form, so students can refer to it when using online resources.

Sample Checklist

This checklist was adapted from Kathy Schrock's "The Five W's of Website Evaluation."

- ☐ **Who**: Who wrote the website? What makes this person an expert in the subject?
- ☐ **What:** Look at the content of the website. Are there many advertisements? Can you get around the site easily? What kinds of information are included: are they facts or opinions? Do you understand what the site is for?
- ☐ **When:** Can you find out when the site was created? When was it last updated?
- ☐ **Where:** Is it easy to figure out where the information came from? Where can you find out more about this website? Does it have a sponsor site? What is the address of the site—is it a *.com*?
- ☐ **Why:** Why is this information useful? How does this information compare to the information from a book on the same topic? Why do you think this page is better than other ones on the same topic?

Debrief

In this world of instant information, students need to have a tool that encourages them to think critically about validity and bias when researching online. This routine must be explicitly referred to and reinforced every time students go online.

> This routine should follow a lesson about the importance of evaluating websites and about Internet safety. See Kathy Schrock's Guide to Everything "Critical Evaluation of Information" (http://www.schrockguide.net/critical-evaluation.html), which has resources and activities around building information literacy with digital sources. Another excellent resource is My WebCHECK (http://www.mywebcheck.net/) created by Marilyn Arnone and Ruth Small, an online evaluation tool that helps students assess the validity of a website. There are four levels of WebCHECK instruments for different grade levels.

Routines for Working Memory

"The more ways something is learned, the more memory pathways are built."
—Judy Willis

Every day we are exposed to a barrage of information. Written instructions, verbal instructions, story books, class novels, class textbooks, newspapers, Twitter feeds, e-mail, Internet content, TV shows, video game instructions—in a single day, we take in approximately 174 newspapers' worth of information. As teachers, we need to be consistent in the ways we share information and help students develop strategies to share and gather the information they are regularly exposed to in our classrooms.

Working memory—our brain's ability to maintain information while using it to complete a task—makes all the difference to successful learning. Research has shown that, as educators, we can help students train their brains and improve their working memory to an age-appropriate level (working memory varies greatly among different age groups). For students with poor working memory, using explicit routines that help them boost their memory recall is essential to their learning.

> **Quick Strategies to Support Working Memory**
>
> - Ask comprehension questions during reading and at the end of reading.
> - Model question-asking, and then encourage students to ask the questions.
> - Start an activity or task with a challenging question or a surprise to pique curiosity.
> - Provide opportunities to repeat and review information.
> - Use rhymes, songs, movements, patterns, and mnemonic devices as cues for retrieving information.
> - For multi-step instructions, include a visual or a checklist, or use discrete steps when performing the task as a group.
> - Use a "sum it up" signal during class lessons, and have a few students briefly summarize what they've learned or explored.

- Encourage students to draw or visualize images related to a new topic.
- Whenever possible, make connections between new topics and known subjects.
- Take a "brain rest" when students become fidgety or distracted. Incorporating physical movement or a short game into the activity allows the brain time to process the new information.

What Page?!

Objective:
To review previous skills and make math equations more authentic.
Key Words: academic, assessment
Suggested Grades: Early Primary/ Primary/Junior/Middle

- When it comes time for all students to open a book to the same page (i.e. a shared reading piece, math page in a textbook, or agenda to fill out), post the page number using math skills you have taught or want to build.
- Examples of ways to get to the page number: math equations; coins (number of cents); tally marks; words; a clock (for page 1–12).

Debrief

This simple review quickly demonstrates how math equations are important in everyday life. This is also my favorite space to review concepts covered long ago that might need a brush-up. If someone is on the wrong page, you can use the moment for quick assessment, review, and skill-building.

Sample Page Postings

1. Open your books.

2. Turn to page $\overline{(3×3)} 1$

3. Read it quietly.

Go to page ||||| ||||| ||

Words I Wonder About

Objectives:
To help students authentically contribute to creating a word wall.
Key Words: curiosity, academic, independence
Suggested Grades: Primary/Junior/ Middle

- Free up a large bulletin board; hang a resealable bag with small paper strips and a few writing utensils on or near it.
- Every time you encounter a challenging or interesting word in your class reading, ask a student to add it to the WIWA (Words I Wonder About) board.
- When correcting students' work, circle commonly misspelled words and mark *WIWA* beside each one. The WIWA acts as an invitation for the student to correctly spell the word and add it to the WIWA board.
- Use WIWA words to supplement your regular spelling program. They can be integrated into spelling words or included as challenge words.

- Use WIWA words for a spelling lesson by having students sort them by syllables or alphabetically. Use them for a grammar lesson by having students sort them into word families or parts of speech.

Debrief

I've tried independent personal dictionaries, but found it hard to maintain thirty different word lists. My students respond to the visual of the exploding word wall, and they love adding challenging words and ones I've found in their personal writing.

To-Do Lists

Objectives:
To help students organize information.
Key Words: self-regulation, independence
Suggested Grades: Early Primary/ Primary/Junior/Middle

- Keep a small supply of to-do list templates; for younger children, use chart paper.
- When beginning a learning task that has multiple steps, describe the learning task in full. Ask students to brainstorm the steps needed to get from the beginning to the end of the task.
- Have students create a to-do list, independently or as a group.
- Where appropriate, add time guidelines beside each step.
- As students work their way through the task, encourage them to check off the items on the to-do list. When using chart paper, students can write their names on sticky notes and move them from step to step.

Debrief

Few children can motor through a complicated multi-step learning activity without needing cues. When they work together to create to-do lists, students have visual cues, written cues, and verbal cues to help guide their way.

Highlight for Meaning

Objective:
Students highlight key words to understand the nature of the task.
Key Words: independence, academic
Suggested Grades: Primary/Junior/ Middle

- When reading questions or instructions, ask students to identify the words that will be key to understanding the task.
- Highlight these words with a highlighter or by underlining key words.
- Revisit the goal of the task.

Debrief

We often introduce highlighting as part of note-taking, but I like to use it all the time to help bring attention to written tasks or questions. Slowing down to read carefully for meaning helps students decipher what the goal of the task is, and also can encourage unsure students to ask for support.

ThinkMarks

Objective:
To provide students with a tool to use in their daily reading.
Key Words: critical thinking, reflection
Suggested Grades: Primary/Junior/ Middle

- Create your own ThinkMark bookmark or use the template on page 59. The book title and student's name go on the back of the ThinkMark.
- Consider what big ideas you want students to be digging for during their reading. Mark them on the ThinkMark.
- Model how to link the ThinkMark with a read-aloud.
- When you discuss text in your class, refer to the terms of the ThinkMark.

ThinkMarks

THINKMARK
CHAPTERS _____ to _____
Sum It Up
What happened?

_____
_____
_____

Up Next
What are your predictions for the
rest of the book?

_____
_____
_____

Connections and Questions
Connect your reading to you, the world,
or another book. Record any questions
you wonder about.

_____
_____
_____
_____

THINKMARK
CHAPTERS _____ to _____
Sum It Up
What happened?

_____
_____
_____

Up Next
What are your predictions for the
rest of the book?

_____
_____
_____

Connections and Questions
Connect your reading to you, the world,
or another book. Record any questions
you wonder about.

_____
_____
_____
_____

THINKMARK
CHAPTERS _____ to _____
Sum It Up
What happened?

_____
_____
_____

Up Next
What are your predictions for the
rest of the book?

_____
_____
_____

Connections and Questions
Connect your reading to you, the world,
or another book. Record any questions
you wonder about.

_____
_____
_____
_____

THINKMARK
CHAPTERS _____ to _____
Sum It Up
What happened?

_____
_____
_____

Up Next
What are your predictions for the
rest of the book?

_____
_____
_____

Connections and Questions
Connect your reading to you, the world,
or another book. Record any questions
you wonder about.

_____
_____
_____
_____

Pembroke Publishers ©2015 *Classroom Routines for Real Learning* by Jennifer Harper and Kathryn O'Brien ISBN 978-1-55138-297-5

Debrief

Unlike large classroom visuals, the ThinkMark is an immediate tool for students to access while reading, and it can remind them about tools to use to help them develop their critical reading strategies. You can photocopy ThinkMarks on colorful cardstock to help them last longer. Consider having students help create their own ThinkMarks using guiding questions and cues they know will help them become more careful readers.

Always Analogies

Objective:
To assist students in connecting new information to a familiar topic or known information.
Key Words: creativity, curiosity
Suggested Grades: Early Primary/ Primary/Junior/Middle

- When introducing a new topic, find an analogy. For example, if you are exploring the body, you might ask students how a cell could be compared to a factory; if you are studying animal migration, compare it to a student's vacation.
- Investigate picture books that can be used as extended analogies: e.g., *Weslandia* for an analogy for early society; *Tough Cookie* for an analogy for life in a city.
- Use a brainstorming web to help explore the analogies.
- Allow time for students to interact with the analogy, to find new connections and comparisons.

Debrief

Analogies are a favorite on standardized tests, but taking an analogy a step further as a brainstorming web helps students explore the new topic by comparing it to a familiar concept. Research has shown that using analogies helps students move information from their working memory to long-term memory.

Wonder Notebooks

Objective:
To encourage students to ask questions and to motivate them to take their learning in their own hands.
Key Words: creativity, critical thinking, student-driven, curiosity
Suggested Grades: Early Primary/ Primary/Junior/Middle

This inspiring routine was developed by teacher Steph Donovan.

- As part of homework, entry time, or a chunk carved out of the day, have students maintain a Wonder notebook.
- In their Wonder notebooks, have students ask open-ended questions that they are truly interested in knowing the answer to.
- Set out the criteria or framework for answering the question, including

    1. recording prior knowledge
    2. recording research gathered
    3. summarizing the answer in a paragraph

- Modify the requirements to complement the skills you are covering in class, such as research, fiction writing (using research in a story), poetry.

Debrief

The Wonder notebook truly empowers students. They get to ask the questions they want, and feel inspired to think about big ideas. You can link their questions to curriculum by using them to work on paragraph writing, taking jot notes, or completing one question a month on a unit of study.

Routines for Self-Advocating

Students who learn to self-advocate acquire a lifelong skill that helps build relationships, confidence, and social flexibility. In a classroom, learning how to ask for help in a positive way shifts the focus from the dependent student to the independent student. Routines that build self-advocacy can foster a more positive relationship between teacher and student, and can lessen the anxiety many students encounter when they are unsure of a concept or situation.

Personal Learning Profiles

Objective:
Students create learning profiles that reflect their learning strengths and needs.
Key Words: reflection, resilience
Suggested Grades: Early Primary/Primary/Junior/Middle

- Emphasize that, in one classroom, everyone will have differences in their abilities. With older students, this might involve a frank conversation about learning strengths and areas to work on. For younger students, it might be more of a generalized commentary on being different from someone else.
- Give each student a list of the areas he/she might need to focus on. Tell students that the list is their personal learning profile. Keep it in a place where the students can access it occasionally (such as a portfolio, or taped inside a journal).

Sample Learning Profile

Terminology	My Strength	Area to Work On
Learning		
Reading		
Processing		
Attention		
Writing		

- Create a chart with strategies and supports that can be used to overcome challenges identified in Area to Work On. Keep this chart in a visible spot.
- When a lesson or activity incorporates areas that will affect one or many learning needs, remind students to think of their profile and look at the chart for support suggestions.

Debrief

Learning profiles give students the words to help describe their needs, and posting a chart with strategies reminds them they can advocate for what they need.

> *One student who had a difficult time focusing became very vocal about classmates who were distracting when she was working. Her peers, understanding that this was a way they could support her, worked to quiet down and not have discussions when it was independent work time.*

Q&A Time

Objective:
To handle students' requests for clarification.
Key Words: academic, curiosity, critical thinking
Suggested Grades: Early Primary/ Primary/Junior/Middle

- When students are working on independent work, set a timer for 10 or 15 minutes (depending on the length of the task).
- At the sound of the timer, begin the question and answer period.
- Encourage students to ask questions about their work (see Bad and Good Questions box below). Remind them that the purpose of Q&A Time is not to share interesting information or to invite discussion or debate, which should be saved for longer class discussions.
- Teachers can lead the Q&A or invite students to lead.
- If there are many keen questioners, use a method, such as Pick-Me Sticks (see page 81), to regulate how many questions are asked.

Debrief

When students see other students ask questions, the classroom becomes a supportive environment for helping each other. Usually, our Q&A period lasts for a few minutes and then students resume working. Often after the Q&A period, students will approach me with other questions or for additional support.

Bad and Good Questions

Some people say there is no such thing as a bad question. It is very likely those people are not teachers. There are bad questions: questions designed to derail the conversation ("What would happen if there was anarchy and then food disappeared?"); questions that are easily solved independently ("Teacher, what do I do? My pencil isn't sharpened"); questions asked solely as a means for people to hear themselves talk ("Teacher, did you just say we have Book Club today?"); and so on. At the start of the year, I spend time talking to my class about different kinds of questions and what are we trying to accomplish by asking the different kinds of questions we ask.

For Q&A periods, focus on the following kinds of questions:

- Next-step questions: what you need to know about the next step of a task.
- Right-there questions: when you need a specific fact or piece of information to understand a topic or idea.
- Clarification questions: when you are unclear about what you are supposed to do or what a piece of information means.

Routines for Creating a Productive Working Environment

We all have different ideas of what a productive level of noise and activity may be. I've been told, both as a compliment and as a critique, that my threshold for volume and movement is high. Keeping that in mind, I started to have conversations with my students to gauge what kind of classroom they need to help them get work done. Their answers range from "absolutely silent" to "I like to dance while I work." Finding a middle ground between these two extremes is important in fostering a sense of respect within the classroom. I knew I had found success when I overheard one student telling another peer, "You need to lower your voice. I remember Neeshan said that he needs it to be quiet when he is writing his story."

10-to-2

Objective:
To structure activities to optimally make use of students' attention spans.
Key Word: self-regulation
Suggested Grades: Early Primary/ Primary/Junior/Middle

- Consider the average attention span of your students. Some research suggests the brain can focus on one task for 7 to 10 minutes; other experts use the guideline of one minute per year (i.e., a five-year-old can focus for 5 minutes).
- As you create activities, use a timed ratio of work to break. For example, if you are reading, giving instructions, or discussing a topic with nine-year-old students, you might use a 10-to-2 ratio: students focus for 10 minutes, and then spend 2 minutes doing a quick partner check-in or some kind of physical movement before continuing.

Debrief

When not doing a hands-on learning task or an independent activity, a 10-to-2 ratio helps sustain the focus of the class. Even when the class seems very engaged in conversation or the reading, make time for a short two-minute refresher, during which they can be moving or more actively involved in learning.

STOP

Objective:
To create a cue for students to work with minimal noise.
Key Words: self-regulation, community-building, motivation
Suggested Grades: Early Primary/ Primary/Junior/Middle

- During an activity that requires no discussion, post a STOP sign on your board (or write the word *Stop*).
- When a student talks, one letter on the sign gets covered or erased.
- If students are able to work in sustained silence, letters can be reinstated.
- If, at the end of the activity, STOP has been completely erased, consider a consequence for the class. If STOP is still on the board, consider some kind of motivator.

Debrief

This routine might seem draconian, but it works very effectively at many age levels. The removal of the letters triggers a wave of silence in my classroom. The students work like a team to keep the letters up and earn back any lost letters.

Noise Checks

Objective:

To help students determine an acceptable level of noise during independent task time.

Key Words: community-building, student-driven

Suggested Grades: Early Primary/ Primary/Junior/Middle

- At the start of an activity, designate one or two students to be noise checkers. These individuals will be responsible for checking the volume of the class.
- At different points during the independent activity, tap one of the noise checkers.
- The noise checker chooses a student in a different area of the classroom. The noise checker calls that person's name and says a random word. It is important that the noise check be done at conversational volume.
- The student chosen must say back the random word. If he/she is unable to hear the word, activity needs to stop and all students need to focus their attention for a short period before resuming their work.

Debrief

After I spent years of *shhh*-ing people, noise checks gave me a fun way to keep the volume low. I am very clear with students that, if the student chosen by the noise checker does not hear the word, it is the responsibility of the class, not the individual, to maintain an environment in which everyone can work.

Countdown Timer

Objective:

For students to self-manage the start of a lesson.

Key Words: self-regulation, motivation

Suggested Grades: Early Primary/ Primary/Junior/Middle

This routine was shared by teacher Mark Ferley.

- Post a countdown timer where it is visible to all students.
- Outline exactly what students need to achieve prior to the lesson.
- Start the lesson precisely when the countdown ends.

Debrief

Prior to using this system, I found myself constantly saying, "You have 20 seconds to be ready." A few students would consistently challenge this, or struggle to get ready in 20 seconds. With a visual timer, students can gauge their time and get ready at their own pace, and I can start my lesson exactly on time.

Ninja Training

Objective:

To provide a physical routine for transition time or when movement is needed.

Key Words: motivation, self-regulation

Suggested Grades: Early Primary/ Primary/Junior/Middle

- Put together an age-appropriate series of three or four physical exercises that require a small amount of space; e.g., jumping jacks, squats, running on the spot, touching toes, stretching from side to side, push-ups, etc.
- Show the exercises to students, with a focus on being mindful of other people's space and on their own form.
- On the cue "Ninja Training," students do 10 repetitions of each exercise and then sit down.

Debrief

Similar to Brain Break (page 43), this routine encourages physical movement. I have been known to call out, "Ninja Training" when we are on a field trip, when students have missed recess, or during tests. Having an opportunity to move around helps students return to their work in a more focused and productive way.

Routines for Homework Success

Homework is a hot topic: some educators are passionately for it, and others against it. This section suggests routines to make homework manageable for both you and your students, if you assign it.

Write it Out

Objective:
For students to effectively use agendas.
Key Words: student-driven, community-building, self-regulation
Suggested Grades: Primary/Junior/ Middle

- Create a space in your classroom for homework to be displayed. Ensure that the homework board replicates the agenda or document students use to track their homework: i.e., the same number of lines, the same structure.
- Empower students to add to the board or to take away items as the day progresses.
- At the end of the day, keep 10 to 15 minutes to review what students are expected to complete at home, how to write it in the agenda, and the due date.
- As homework is collected in the morning, use the board as a tool to review missing work. Continue to modify the board to ensure it is easy to understand.
- Circulate and check each agenda. This is an ideal space for stamps or stickers: e.g., to show homework has been checked and levelled, to check that it was copied correctly.

Debrief

Agendas are not new. Many schools have them, but how they are used can vary. They can be a good tool for student empowerment and self-management. They can also literally be heavy burdens on students, weighing down their backpacks. If we want to ensure that students take part in home communication and that their voices are valued, then we need to trust them and empower them through the agenda. They need to know that what they write is important.

Agenda Stamp: Self-Regulator

Objective:
To empower students to manage their homework and the use of their agendas.
Key Words: motivation, independence
Suggested Grades: Junior/Middle

- Create a ticket, card, or sticker that can be proudly displayed. Write on it *Self-Regulator.*
- Routinely check students' agendas and track homework completion.
- If a student completes the agenda perfectly and consistently returns his/her homework, make note of it.
- After five checks, that student earns the title of *Self Regulator.* The sign can be proudly displayed and serves as a reminder that you don't need to check this agenda.

Debrief

Similar to the *Never to Be Checked Again* desk system, this routine allows students to show their independence. But to do this, they need to understand what a perfect agenda looks like and how to achieve it. They also need to participate in the tracking, to understand what they need to do to improve and how close they are to demonstrating self-regulation of homework routines.

What I Learned Today

Objective:
For each student to share.
Key Words: reflection, assessment
Suggested Grades: Early Primary/
Primary/Junior/Middle

- Provide a space in the agenda or a separate notebook for each student to write a quick sentence or thought to sum up what they took away from the day; e.g., a big idea, an "a-ha" moment, or an incident.

Debrief

This works well as a daily routine, but might need changing up once in a while. You can use this routine as a weekly reflection. Giving students the chance to reflect in class helps us understand what they take away from the lesson/day/week. It also provides a platform on which parents can start conversations at home.

CHAPTER 5

Working Collaboratively

School is the ultimate social experience and this atmosphere shapes our students. It is the space where students learn academics—and so much more. Education fosters growth. In our vibrant and busy classroom full of individuals, students need to negotiate, find their space, and learn to get along to survive. We want and need them to thrive in a rich classroom community where they feel safe. Once they feel safe, we need them to challenge themselves and each other, ultimately pushing toward a richer understanding of themselves as learners.

Once students have left the education system, they can choose to work in private spaces or in isolation. But before that, they need to work and develop in a populated space. This chapter explores the different grouping possibilities in our classroom that allow us to create a dynamic collaborative environment.

Collaboration requires working toward a common goal. It is more than just a series of bodies trying to avoid conflict in a confined space. We all know there is no *i* in team. That being said, the purpose of putting students in groups is for them to refine what they think using knowledge gained from others. Each individual joins a group with the expectation that they will

- listen
- add ideas
- challenge/question others' ideas to compare and build on what they think
- reform their ideas
- come out with a stronger understanding

With that end in mind, we must ask ourselves: What do we want our students to learn? What are the outcomes or objectives? The next step is to take the answers to these questions and apply them to our students. What do we know about their learning style? How do they learn best? Finally, we have to determine if the skill or learning objective is best suited for small-group learning.

When we place our students in groups, we multiply the amount of interaction they are required to produce. In a whole-class lesson, we might lose our shy students, since fewer voices are needed to continue the flow of the lesson. But in smaller groups, our students are more accountable to each other and required to increase their participation to complete the task.

Researchers report that, regardless of subject matter, students working in small groups tend to learn more of what is taught and retain it longer than when the same content is presented in other instructional formats. Students who work in collaborative groups also appear more satisfied with their classes (Stevens and Slavin, 1992). In a classroom, you will generally find three different types of collaborative work:

- Informal groups are formed when you ask students to turn to their "neighbor" to reflect on a question or problem.
- Formal groups are created to work together on a specific task or project. These groups often are maintained on a long-term basis.
- Study teams work together on several different tasks and are expected to support and mentor each other through their group work. Examples of study teams might include book club groups, groups for math extension programs, and peer editing partners.

There are many different ways to group students together for collaborative work. Each way has its own advantages and disadvantages.

Ability Groups: students grouped together by their academic ability.
Pros: Having students working with peers of a similar ability can allow for extension, and it can help a teacher target support for struggling students.
Cons: In homogenous groups, students will not have the modelling provided by peers of different abilities; as well, ability groups can create stigmas within a classroom, categorizing "smart" and "dumb" students.

Personality Types: students grouped together by their social and emotional skills and needs.
Pros: Considering who works well with others can encourage a more effective social dynamic in a group.
Cons: Grouping students by their personality might mean that more affable students always find themselves working with students who are more challenging socially.

Personal Choice: students choose who they wish to work with.
Pros: Students are often more motivated when they can choose their own partners.
Cons: Students can be left out and feel isolated if they are not grouped with their "chosen" friend; also, groups might be created that do not create positive working environments.

Student Interest: students are grouped by their interests; for example, in a book club, students select the book and the group is formed through this choice.
Pros: Students have an interest in the topic they are exploring.
Cons: The group might not be balanced academically or socially.

What Is the Ideal Group Size?

Common practice around collaborative learning points to groups of three to five students. The larger the group size, the more difficult it is to organize tasks, manage different skills, and reach consensus.

There are apps (such as Make My Groups or Team Shake) and programs (Microsoft Excel or SMART Notebook) that electronically group students. Many are designed to appear random, but they also offer the option of secretly tagging your students to ensure groups work well.

Routines for Grouping

The first step in the process of collaboration is grouping our students. As listed above, there are various ways that we can group our students.

Individual Choice

Objective:
To allow the class to create groups based on interest in activities.
Key Word: motivation
Suggested Grades: Early Primary/ Primary/Junior/Middle

- Share with the class the stations or activities they will need to work at.
- Explain to students that they need to think carefully about the station they will be working at as well as who is at the station. It is important for them to understand that they cannot pick stations based on a peer's choice.
- Place each student's name on a stick or piece of paper.
- Pull a stick or piece of paper and let that student select a station/activity.

Debrief

Allowing students to start their activities/stations randomly works best for rotations or in situations in which everyone does not need to complete each activity.

Choice Based on Need

Objective:
To provide students with choice as to what activity they would like to complete, based on the skills they want to work on.
Key Words: self-regulation, assessment, independence
Suggested Grades: Junior/Middle

- Show students the stations around the room and what to do at each one.
- Explain and clearly label the skill to be taught or reviewed at each station.
- Outline the time allotment for the stations—how long they have to complete all stations and how to divide that into time at individual stations—if they feel the need to work at all of them.
- Let students go to the stations based on their self-identified need. Circulate to ensure that everyone understands the tasks.
- As students complete a station, have them leave their name or track their completion. This will allow students who are completing the task later to ask peers for assistance.

Debrief

I use this technique the day before a math test and during guided reading breakout sessions. This style of group work succeeds if students already know the required skills and are practicing. They can move fluidly from station to station, practicing at their own pace. In essence, this rotation is very fluid and can be considered independent; however, while at a station, students often strengthen their understanding based on conversations and collaborative work with peers.

Student Input

Objective:
For students to feel their voice is heard in group-making.
Key Words: independence, self-regulation, student-driven
Suggested Grades: Primary/Junior/ Middle

- Explain the task that is required. Students will need to understand the end result to determine who would be an appropriate partner.
- Explain to students that they will need to pick a partner or some people that they believe they will be able to work with to complete the task.
- If you have done individual assessments on personality types, reference this and suggest that students consider a variety of learning styles when deciding on pairs.
- Have students justify why they feel they should work with the peer they choose.
- If the partner selection is done on paper or privately, offer students the opportunity to include any concerns they might have with other students.
- Use student partner grouping to make larger groups of four.

Debrief

Providing students with a voice in grouping is ideal for larger group projects. However, it is important that students fully understand that they might not get their choice. They might be selected by someone else, and that person could have a stronger argument. Often students feel more content to be chosen than to get the partner they requested.

I received these sticky notes in response to the question "What aboriginal group would you like to study?" Many students were flexible and stated, "any." However, these two reminded me to always provide a space for my students' voices.

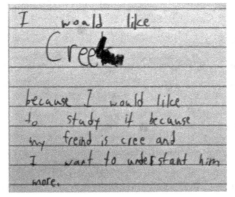

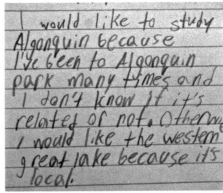

Quick Groups

Objective:
Students quickly sort themselves into pairs for quick activities that require a partner.
Key Words: independence, student-driven
Suggested Grades: Early Primary/Primary/Junior/Middle

- Have each student find a space in the classroom. If possible, remove them from their desks and get them to move around, so that they are exposed to students who are usually outside of arms reach.
- Ask students to find a partner who
  - they have never worked with before
  - they do not play or socialize with outside of school
  - is the opposite gender
  - is born in the same month or season
  - is wearing the same color
  - has a last name (or first) with the same number of syllables as their own
  … and the list goes on!

Debrief

These quick groups can be very successful in combining students who would not normally select each other. Because the task is small, it gives them the chance to connect and build a relationship in a less stressful environment.

> *To form groups for script writing, the students in my Grade 7 drama class first completed a character survey analysis, recording their character traits in order of strength. This data is vital for many teachers in understanding students' motivations, approach, etc. But to explore how traits can both empower them and need monitoring, students chose a partner with a conflicting trait to work with to write a script.. Many realizations came forward, including "Humor is not always appropriate. It can be awkward when someone is sharing a passion that is serious."*

Routines for Small-Group Monitoring

Using routines from the last section, we know that a group is interacting and collaborating well. They are getting along. But are they getting anything done? These routines help us keep our groups on track, know where they are, and find out what assistance they might need next. This section is all about the ongoing monitoring of groups.

Each of the routines in this section is public and visible to each student and group in the class. This is intentional. If the classroom is a collaborative space where our students are learning from each other, then we need to provide them with access and information to enable this collaboration. Our students need to know what other groups have completed or are working on as a resource; they can seek out assistance from or ask questions of groups that have finished the task, or they can reach out to groups that seem stuck. For our classroom to be truly collaborative, students need to feel free to access all resources—teachers, books, technology, and each other.

Linear Flow Chart

Objective:

To use a flow chart to track progress through linear activities.

Key Words: community-building, assessment, self-regulation

Suggested Grades: Early Primary/ Primary/Junior/Middle

- Use this for linear tasks; i.e., tasks in which everyone completes the same steps in the same order, such as the writing process or steps in a presentation.
- Create a basic flow chart outlining the key job title, station title, or description of the task.
- Label a clothespin, or other tracking device, with each group name.
- Place the pins on the flow chart. The groups move their pins as they complete the tasks.

Debrief

A clear visual flow chart is a wonderful tool to track what tasks groups have completed and what stage they are at. It also gives students an opportunity to check in with other groups about the task: if they have questions, if they would like to see a sample to build on, if they need redirection. Posting a flow chart makes the classroom collaborative, as students can build on each other's experiences. This routine also be used for rotational tasks. If the flow is rotational or web-based, each group leaves a trail of checkmarks, stickers, etc. as it moves through the tasks.

Rotational Checklist

Objective:

To enable students to seek assistance from each other in rotational tasks.

Key Words: community-building, assessment, self-regulation

Suggested Grades: Early Primary/ Primary/Junior/Middle

- Use this for rotational tasks; i.e., tasks in which everyone completes the same steps at different stages, such as centres, reading groups, or math stations.
- Post a list of the activities that need to be completed. Across the top or bottom, list the groups.
- As a group completes the activity, have them place a checkmark on the task.

Debrief

This system of group management and collaboration works best if each group needs to complete the same tasks.

For tasks that require one answer or a set solution and that suit a bit of competition, this activity can be modified to push our learners, as long as it does not affect the creative flow. Create a system of levelled checkmarks; e.g., regular checkmark for task completion and bold checkmark to demonstrate an exemplary model. Students will know which groups to seek out, and will go to ones that created the exemplary model. As well, they will be motivated to achieve the higher level. If you are able to balance the class so that each group receives a bold checkmark for one task, then you have an instant presentation and collaborative space where all students can share the work in which they shined.

Web-Based Flow

Objective:
To monitor the movement and progress of groups.
Key Words: motivation, self-regulation, student-driven, critical thinking
Suggested Grades: Primary/Junior/ Middle

- Use this routine when groups are not required to complete the same task.
- Post a list of groups or group names.
- As students finish a task, have them record what they have done in three words or less below their group name. If you are using an interactive whiteboard, you can clone activity icons for the students to easily drag them to their groups

Debrief

This system allows for critical thinking, as students need to summarize the main idea of what they just did. In addition, the flexibility of creating an open space allows groups to design tasks they feel meet the needs of the assignment.

Routines for Reaching Consensus

One of the biggest hurdles in collaborative learning is helping students meld their different ideas together. Consensus can be the emergence of the loudest and bossiest idea or, with modelled routines, consensus can be reached through discussions by which students take the most interesting and powerful pieces of their ideas and bring them together with the ideas of their peers.

Call It Democracy

Objective:
To come to a consensus in a traditional democracy.
Key Words: community-building, student-driven
Suggested Grades: Early Primary/ Primary/Junior/Middle

- Create a brainstorming chart. Add ideas as the students come up with them. List as many as you can.
- When the ideas are listed, ask students to select their top ideas. Choose the number students select so you can move through the list at a decent rate.
- Use the blind vote system—students keep heads down and raise a hand when you call one of their chosen ideas—to narrow down until you have the last remaining choices.

Debrief

This system works very well when creating a collaborative piece, such as a play or story, naming a class pet, or assigning jobs in the classroom. But be warned: the democratic way, as much as it is empowering, can get tiresome if overused.

Mash Up

Objective:
To encourage students to consider different ideas for a group project or activity.
Key Words: reflection, creativity, curiosity
Suggested Grades: Junior/Middle

- Outline the goal of the task.
- Give each student a sticky note or scrap piece of paper. Ask each student to write one way or idea related to the goal.
- Students bring their ideas to the group. Write the goal in the middle of a piece of chart paper or large space (like a chalkboard), around which students sort their ideas. Similar ideas will be grouped together, and any different ideas are left on their own.
- At this point, the group might choose to go with the ideas that are similar, or you might challenge them to find connections between the different ideas. For example, if students are looking at ways to present their information, and one student wants to do a poster while another wants to do a board game, encourage them to consider a way to combine the two—a poster that serves as the base for a game?

Debrief

Encouraging students to look for connections among different ideas is a great way to spark creative thinking, as it forces them to move beyond the easy ideas.

Group Goals

Objective:
To focus the direction of the group and to highlight the objectives and goals of the group.
Key Words: empathy, reflection, student-driven
Suggested Grades: Junior/Middle

- At the start of a period of group work, have every group create a list of group goals. Each member of the group can contribute a goal. Goals can be work-related or social-emotional.
- Older students must be able to explain why the goal is important to them.
- The final goal to be determined is how the group will reach consensus. Some ideas: Will they take a group vote? Will one person choose each time? Will they flip a coin? Will they do a draw?

Debrief

Yes, students have to reach consensus on how they reach consensus. The most popular way to reach consensus seems to be a vote or using rock, paper, scissors. Depending on the type of collaborative work, having a predetermined plan for how to reach consensus allows students to move forward and accomplish the task within a given time frame. For book clubs, I've found setting group goals very effective.

Routines to Ensure Individual Accountability

Putting our students in groups and tracking their progress does not stop some students from taking over or others from letting it happen. These routines were created to track and encourage fair contributions from all group members.

Active Listening

Objective:
To clearly model active listening.
Key Words: community-building, assessment
Suggested Grades: Early Primary/Primary

- At the beginning of the year, have the class define what active listening looks like: making eye contact, listening, ability to summarize what the speaker has said.
- Create a class set of cards: see sample on page 74.

- When the students are working in pairs, each assumes a card, either the ear or the mouth. If they have the ear, they need to be an active listener. If they have the mouth, they can share their ideas.

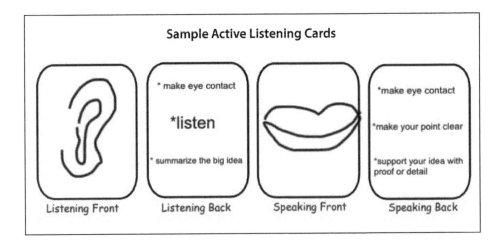

Debrief

Listening is key to working in any collaborative environment. As the year goes on, these cards will become less necessary, as students begin to actively listen without them. But keep them handy. They are the perfect tools for when students come into the class after a rough recess, when they are caught up in frustration and need a reminder that active listening is needed to solve problems.

What's My Role?

- As groups are settling in, create roles or jobs for each member. The roles can be self-explanatory, or can come with a quick description.

Objective:
To assign each student a role in the group for fair participation.
Key Words: community-building, motivation
Suggested Grades: Primary/Junior/ Middle

Here are some roles that work well for many groups:

- Materials Manager obtains and returns all materials to teacher.
- Recorder writes down everything the group discusses and completes any paper to be submitted to the teacher. This task works well in rotation, to maintain interest.
- Speaker of the House keeps the group on task, focused, and responsible for not talking about other topics; also navigates whose turn it is to talk next and keeps the flow of the conversation going.
- Time Manager keeps track of the time and makes sure the group finished the activity in the allotted time.
- Interpreter is the only person allowed to talk to the teacher; must convey all questions from the group to the teacher.
- Question Asker is responsible for creating and asking open-ended questions of the group to keep the conversation going.
- Reporter shares with the whole class what the group has done or discussed.

Debrief

Roles in groups work very well when the task is one lesson long, or not too extensive. However, when the group is required to sustain their collaborative learning longer, we suggest rotating the roles within the group to ensure that the students keep fresh and interested in their group learning experience.

Talking Sticks

Objective:
To encourage every member of a group to speak during discussions.
Key Words: independence, motivation, student-driven
Suggested Grades: Early Primary/Primary/Junior/Middle

- At the start of a group discussion, every member of the group gets a predetermined number (three or four) of craft sticks or counters. These are talking sticks.
- As the group participates in discussion, a group member puts a talking stick in a central area each time he/she speaks.
- Once a group member has used up his/her talking sticks, he/she must wait until other group members have had an equal opportunity to share.
- Once everyone has shared and no one has talking sticks left, the sticks can be redistributed.

Debrief

I use talking sticks during book club discussions, as I find it helps create a balance between those students who are very comfortable sharing and those students who need prompting.

Routines for Individual Assessment

Working in groups is vital for our students to learn how to negotiate and collaborate, how to solve problems and create solutions. However, even in these moments, we want to ensure that every individual in the group has space to be heard, and we want to hear what they have to say so that we can help facilitate their learning.

Colored Writing

Objective:
To identify the individual contributions in a collaborative written activity.
Key Words: self-regulation, assessment
Suggested Grades: Early Primary/Primary/Junior/Middle

- Provide each student with a colored pencil or marker.
- As the activity develops, that student writes only with that writing tool.

Debrief

This routine allows the student to have accountability in a group activity. The color coding system can remain your secret, so that you can monitor contributions. This activity also extends nicely into book talks or other group activities with set roles.

Anonymous Assessment

Objective:
Using a survey to gather
    information about how a
    group's inner dynamic is
    working.
Key Words: self-regulation,
    motivation, assessment
Suggested Grades: Junior/Middle

- Provide each student with a survey to complete online or in writing.
- Think about the skills you want to encourage, your survey could include
    Participation (quality and quantity)
    Preparation (collaboration)
    Punctuality (interpersonal skills)
    Respect (interpersonal skills)
    Contribution of ideas (collaboration)
    Creativity (problem-solving)
    Commitment (collaboration)
- Each group member anonymously reports on other group members.
- These notes are shared with you, but kept in confidence.

Debrief

Group participation assessments reminds our students that their involvement in group work is important, and it can be marked. If the task was independently done, or completed outside of school, then peer assessment becomes necessary for you to understand the group dynamic, both for this project and going forward. This routine is also ideal for use in the middle of the project. Providing students with time to work through their relationships and evaluate their group dynamic can keep the group moving forward positively for the duration of the project.

Clipboard Circulator

Objective:
To monitor and share assessment
    tracking of individuals in a
    group situation.
Key Words: motivation, assessment
Suggested Grades: Junior/Middle

- Create a class list as a chart, with space to write around each name. Keep the class list on a clipboard in a visible spot.
- Explain to students that you will use this space to record observational notes on their individual progress and participation.
- When you touch a student's shoulder, or ask him/her, that student can add observational notes beside his/her name. For example, you could say, "Could you please write that you got to task quickly beside your name," or "Could you please add the comment you just made to your peer beside your name."
- Circulate around the room, having students add notes.
- Be open to students who would like to add a note. Ask them for justification.

Debrief

By sharing the coveted clipboard of observations, students become more aware that we are in a social space and they need to monitor their behavior. It keeps off-task students on track and celebrates positive behavior. Open-assessment strategies like this limit questions about marks, as students know what evidence is recorded.

Routines to Develop Listening Skills

Listening is often called the most important language art. Pinnell and Jaggar (2003) cite researchers reporting that people spent as much time listening as they did reading, writing, and speaking combined. Having clear routines to develop the listening skills of all members of a classroom is a critical part of building class community. If students and teachers can listen attentively, critically, and empathetically to one another, the class will grow and flourish.

Finding the Big Idea

Objective:
To encourage the development of efferent listening by helping students identify the key ideas.
Key Words: academic, reflection, critical thinking
Suggested Grades: Junior/Middle

- Before beginning a lesson, let students know that people often give clues to help us identify important ideas.
- Ask students to watch and listen carefully for certain words or nonverbal clues that might indicate important information. Repeating information, key words (such as *important, critical, interesting, key*), raising one's voice for emphasis, using finger signs (such as holding up one finger for "number 1"), and pointing at information are just a few indications that information is important.
- As a class, create a list of different clues people give when discussing the big idea.
- At the end of the lesson or activity, ask a few students to summarize what they learned or experienced.
- Using these summaries, ask a student to share the big idea.

Debrief

This routine works well for peer presentations, and for getting students to focus as well as listen to the teacher.

Finger Signs

Objectives:
To create a list of nonverbal cues for class conversations and other situations.
Key Words: independence, self-regulation
Suggested Grades: Primary/Junior/Middle

- As a class, brainstorm the different ways people try to get each other's attention.
- As everyone is brainstorming, sort ideas into categories as to why we try to get people's attention: e.g., we need something, we don't understand a question, we want to share an idea.
- As a class, create different nonverbal cues to use for different classroom activities and routines; for example, making the *W* shape with the fingers for "I need to go to the washroom."

Debrief

I have found that creating nonverbal cues for the class helps eliminate many silly conversations and encourages student independence. For example, we have a signal for "question" that allows all of us to know when a student has a burning question that needs to be answered so they can move forward with the lesson. Often, other students in the classroom will quietly answer a student's question before I even notice the signal.

Interactive Read-Alouds

- Before beginning a read-aloud, let students know that along the way, you will be pausing for a quick check-in. By setting these parameters at the start, you avoid having students wave their hands frantically throughout the story (and inevitably not listen to the story because they are too excited about sharing).
- Stop at pivotal points in the story to make predictions.
- In sections that are very rich in detail, stop and ask students to close their eyes and visualize what they see. Give them the opportunity to describe their visualizations.
- Have a signal that students can use if they have thought of a connection to the story; e.g., making a *C* with a hand. Pause, when possible, to allow students to share their connections.

> *I use pick-me sticks (see page 81) for our read-aloud chats, as I find all students are keen to participate. Prior to our read-alouds, I usually set these parameters: that a student can share a connection once; that we only listen to two connections at a time; and, once the page has turned, they must think of a new connection.*

Debrief

Build time into your read-aloud to ask students if they have any questions. This time might come at the end of a chapter or a picture book, or midway through a book that you think will inspire much questioning and discussion.

Critical Listening

A routine around critical listening can be introduced only after routines for efferent listening (being able to recognize the big idea, organize and summarize information). Once students are able to identify the key details in a message, they can build their critical listening skills.

- Use news video clips or a piece of literature as an entry point for developing critical listening.
- The following questions help prompt students to evaluate the message beyond the facts. Use prompts, such as
  - What is the speaker or author's message?
  - Is there an emotional appeal to the information?
  - Are the illustrations or photos persuasive?
  - Are propaganda devices being used?

Objective:
Developing a routine around class read-alouds that encourages insightful discussion of the text.
Key Words: academic, reflection
Suggested Grades: Early Primary/ Primary/Junior/Middle

Objective:
To encourage listening for evaluating a message.
Key Words: self-regulation, critical thinking
Suggested Grades: Junior/Middle

Media Smarts is a Canadian charity focused on providing children and youth with critical thinking skills to engage in media. Their website has many resources for educators: http://mediasmarts.ca/

Routines for Collaborative Technology Use

We know that collaboration should be a broad term that applies to all supplies, tools, activities, and anything else in the classroom. However, use of technology in the classroom, be it a small group working on the interactive whiteboard or students eager to grab laptops or tablets, can quickly resemble a zombie apocalypse. Technology seems to have a special allure that shuts down rational thought. In the sheer desire to obtain technology, students seem to lose all notions of collaboration, respect, and personal boundaries. These technology routines are written in the vain attempt to save you in such a situation.

Making the Interactive Whiteboard Interactive

Objective:

To engage the class in making up rules for the interactive whiteboard.

Key Word: community-building

Suggested Grades: Early Primary/ Primary/Junior/Middle

- Break your students into small groups of three to five to take turns at the interactive whiteboard. Give a separate task for groups not on the interactive whiteboard.
- When a group comes to the interactive whiteboard, explain to them that they need to explore what it can do and how it can be useful.
- Have students record their ideas on the interactive whiteboard.

Debrief

Use the resulting list of ideas of what students feel comfortable with, enjoy, and can do on the interactive whiteboard as a platform for preparing and planning tasks.

Rethinking Technology

Objective:

For students to approach technology with a goal and a critical lens.

Key Words: reflection, creativity, critical thinking

Suggested Grades: Early Primary/ Primary/Junior/Middle

- Create a class T-chart. On one side write *Activity* and on the other write *Purpose*.
- Have students brainstorm why they use technology. Each time they come up with an app, game, tool, or product, write it on the Activity side.
- Push students to think about why they are using or creating these tools. What is the purpose of using technology?
- Use the Purpose list as an anchor chart to remind students that they are raising awareness, finding answers, sharing information, motivating others, collaborating, and making a difference.

Debrief

Keep the chart public and refer to it when students type or add to a public space. This conversation nicely complements lessons on digital footprints and digital citizenship.

Playing Out Rules

Objective:
To give students space and time to problem-solve around technology.
Key Words: reflection, critical thinking
Suggested Grades: Junior/Middle

- Have students come up with a series of rules or agreements for technology use.
- Prior to sharing the rules, provide each group of students with one piece of technology to share.
- Have the group work through to determine if their rules or agreements solve problems or create them.
- Give them space to adjust their rules/agreements.

Debrief

Our students are often in the position to make class agreements. They also love rules. However, when they are tempted with an electronic device, do the rules still hold? Are the rules good? Do they need some work? This is an authentic way for students to create and adjust terms that they agree with.

Routines for Student Participation

The participating routines are inspired by Barrie and Noreen Carol Bennett, authors of *Beyond Monet*.

It is very important, when selecting a student to offer a response or share an idea, that the student feels comfortable and supported in the classroom. Building a classroom in which everyone feels safe means understanding that isolating individuals or humiliating them by having them respond without confidence discourages them and limits future risk-taking.

At the same time, the class cannot be represented by a few individuals while the quieter students hide in the background. There needs to be a balance and space for each individual to share, take risks, and shine. These routines are created to manage that delicate balance.

Talk to a Buddy

Objective:
To provide space for students to work through ideas and form their thoughts.
Key Words: community-building, critical thinking
Suggested Grades: Early Primary/ Primary/Junior/Middle

- When asking a question, prior to getting a response or asking for hands, tell students, "Talk to the person next to you."
- Circulate, listen, and pull them onto task.

Debrief

Changing the way we ask questions tracks back to the types of questions we ask. As well as providing our students the space to work out their response, we also need to challenge them with questions worth thinking about. For example, rather than asking, "What is 2 times 5?" we ask, "What are some ways we can make 10?" By encouraging our students to collaborate prior to taking a risk, we strengthen their confidence and give them an opportunity to work through their ideas. This atmosphere takes the focus off the teacher and whether someone is right or wrong, and instead builds a community spirit where ideas are shared and developed.

Ask a Group

Objective:
To pull the class out of a discussion and ask for a voice to represent the collective thoughts.
Key Words: community-building, critical thinking
Suggested Grades: Early Primary/Primary/Junior/Middle

- After students have worked through an idea and discussed their response with a partner, call them together to share.
- When calling on an individual to share, reference the partnership/group; e.g., ask, "Tommy, what did you and Soraya come up with?"

Debrief

When asked for a collaborative response, the student feels two things instantly: less isolated and comforted that he/she is speaking on behalf of a group; and challenged to formulate a response that encompasses many voices.

Pick-Me Sticks

Objective:
To ensure everyone has an equal chance to share their ideas.
Key Words: assessment, community-building
Suggested Grades: Early Primary/Primary/Junior/Middle

- At the beginning of the year, have each student write their name on a pick-me stick, rock, or other small object.
- Place these objects together in a container close to the discussion area.
- When you ask a question, give students time to discuss. When you are ready to call on a student, pick a stick out of the container.
- Ask the student whose name is on the stick what his/her group has come up with.

> There are a variety of smart phone and tablet apps that work like pick-me sticks. For example, Stick Pick and Teacher's Pick are iPad apps that allow you to input student names and keep track of how often that student is being picked or answers a question.

Debrief

The beauty of pick-me sticks is that they instantly get rid of the hands-up. Every student is on an equal playing field and can share ideas. Of course, equal is not necessarily fair, and we strongly support the use of pick-me sticks combined with Talk to a Buddy (page 80) and Ask a Group (above). These three steps for sharing ideas dramatically change the classroom focus from an individual knowing the answer to collaborative building of a stronger answer. Everyone is accountable, yet everyone also feels supported.

CHAPTER 6

Routines for Assessment

In order to help our students achieve, we need to know where they are and where we can guide them next. We want them to take risks and make mistakes to continually grow. And we want them to feel proud of what they achieve. Assessment means that we are providing feedback to keep our students engaged and learning. Routines around assessment are important for teachers, but also for students. Once they know what they will be assessed on, and how, they can build confidence, take risks, and grow. It is the known that creates the comfort to develop, not the unknown.

Assessment can range from a quick check-in that builds a student's learning to that huge pile of assignments that lingers on our desks or cripples our backs as we lug it to our cars. The routines in this chapter cannot eliminate the possibility of large assessment tasks. But we strive to include and balance routines that are efficient, are effective, and offer variety when your back starts aching.

Routines for Assessment *for* Learning

In assessment for learning, we use formative or diagnostic assessment to determine what prior knowledge our students have on the topic.

In this dialogue, teachers ask

- What knowledge are you coming to the table with?
- How can I provide the feedback you need to dive further?
- What further instruction or guidance is needed?

In this dialogue, students ask

- What do I already understand?
- In what direction do I want to head next?
- What am I interested in learning more about?

Understanding what prior knowledge or skills our students bring to a concept is vital for determining where to go next. This does not mean that we are tailoring individual curricula for each student. It does mean that we get a sense of who to challenge, who to support, and who to guide along. When we begin a new concept, our students fall into the following categories:

- Full understanding: they are passionate about the topic and have spent some time learning about it
- Partial understanding: they have some knowledge in bits and pieces
- Little/No understanding: this is new to them
- Misconception: they have a false sense of the concept

Knowledge is an important aspect of assessing for prior knowledge. In addition to knowledge, we also want to get a sense of our students' confidence in the skills we are covering. How do they feel about this new topic? When given a list of the skills, what do they address as a concern?

Popcorn

Objective:
To quickly assess prior knowledge/ misconceptions.
Key Words: community-building, curiosity
Suggested Grades: Early Primary/ Primary/Junior/Middle

- Preface this game by explaining that it is simply to share ideas; this is not a time to correct or question any misconceptions.
- Write or share a discussion prompt, a question about the topic to get the conversation going; e.g., "What do you know about structures?" or "What does multiplication mean?"
- Toss a ball around and call the catcher's name.
- As a student catches the ball, he/she can jump up and share an idea.

Debrief

The ball circulating and popping up makes this activity a great start for wiggly kids who need to move around. Listen as the ideas start to flow and use this information as your basis for your teaching: What are they all keen to share? What do they already know? What misconceptions need addressing?

Activating Prior Knowledge

Objective:
Students consider what they already know about a subject to help them make connections to a new topic.
Key Words: assessment, academic
Suggested Grades: Early Primary/ Primary/Junior/Middle

- Write the topic on the board or in a visible spot in the classroom.
- Give students a quick explanation of the topic or background on it, if necessary. You can do this verbally or by showing students a visual that links to the topic.
- Have the students work in teams to verbally recount all the ideas and facts they think are linked to the topic.
- As a class, share ideas.

> *Sometimes, we orally share our ideas. With topics we will be visiting in great detail, I ask students to record one or two of their ideas on sticky notes and we display these on a moving I Think/I Know board: students begin by adding their sticky notes to the I Think section and, as we do the research or exploring, they move their sticky notes to the I Know section.*

Debrief

Recording prior knowledge on a chart makes a strong visual. The students can add to it as the unit progresses. If you can access an interactive whiteboard, this brainstorm map can be constantly added to and sorted as the concept develops, creating a valuable reference of learning.

Assessing Confidence

Objective:
To assess student confidence with tasks.
Key Word: reflection
Suggested Grades: Primary/Junior/ Middle

- List the tasks and activities that will be used to teach the concept. Explain them to students.

- Use a blind survey, checklist, or clickers for the interactive whiteboard to provide students with a space to share their comfort level with the tasks

Debrief

When we start new units, we assess knowledge: what do our students know about this topic? Then we plan a series of lessons and activities to cover the gaps, push their thinking, and engage them. Understanding our students' confidence level for the activities and tasks (rather than in the topic) can help us prepare them for a stronger product. For instance, rather than finding out what our students know about aboriginal peoples, ask "How do you feel about writing narratives, presenting a monologue, or completing a project with a partner?"

Four Corners

Objective:
To quickly determine prior knowledge.
Key Words: critical thinking, academic
Suggested Grades: Primary/Junior/ Middle

- Post these signs in four separate areas of your room:
  Strongly Agree
  Agree
  Disagree
  Strongly Disagree
- Let students know that the middle of the room is for *I do not have enough information.*
- Ask a question pertaining to the concept you will be studying.
- Have the students commit to a spot in the room.
- If you feel many are making random choices or do not have the full understanding, ask them to justify their position.

Debrief

This quick game gets everyone moving and provides you with key information on what knowledge your students are bringing with them to the concept. This activity also feeds well into an ongoing and summative task, as you can ask questions during and after the learning.

Quick Flash

Objective:
To quickly determine the knowledge students have when approaching the concept.
Key Words: independence, assessment
Suggested Grades: Early Primary/ Primary/Junior

- Provide a space for response; e.g., a hand signal, or a whiteboard flash with the answer.
- Ask a question pertaining to the concept you will be studying; e.g., *What is 5 + 3?* or *What is the role of the government?*
- Have students share their responses instantly by showing their fingers or writing the response on the whiteboard and holding it in the air for you to see.

Debrief

This quick assessment is very engaging, because the pace is fast and it becomes a game. Ensure that students feel comfortable if they have no answer. Controlling when the whiteboards go in the air (at the sound of a bell, or at the count of three) will also help to keep a sense of calm.

Assessment *as* Learning

Assessment as learning takes place during the learning process. Students are active members of this process, as they have to assess their own learning in relation to their learning goals and the criteria for success.

In this dialogue, teachers ask

- What are your learning goals and do they align with the criteria?
- Are you comfortable with how your learning is progressing?
- What feedback or strategies do you need next?

In this dialogue, students ask

- Am I meeting the objectives or big idea for this topic?
- How am I connecting what I already knew to the new knowledge I am gathering?
- How will I incorporate the feedback given to me?
- Where do I refine and where do I go next?

Tools for Assessment as Learning
- diaries, logs, journals
- portfolios
- peer and self-assessment
- goal-setting
- projects
- group work
- profiles
- skills and competencies

Routines for Dealing with Mistakes

Encouraging our students to make mistakes is one of our hardest jobs. Students come to school assuming they need to know the answers and, if they don't, many hesitate to share their ideas. We have all taught those keen students who so rarely make mistakes that they also rarely take risks. And we have seen that, by the time these students are in the middle years, they will stay quiet until absolutely sure of the exact answer. This limits their creativity and exploration, and pulls them back from developing beyond their comfort zone. Making mistakes is vital for moving forward, growing, and learning. These routines are created to help our students take risks and keep moving forward.

Levelled Stamps

Objective:
To provide students with instant feedback, encouraging them to keep trying and learning from their mistakes.
Key Words: motivation, reflection, resilience
Suggested Grades: Early Primary/Primary/Junior/Middle

- Keep a variety of stamps of different themes and sizes.
- For activities that have a correct answer (e.g., printing lessons, math equations, grammar worksheets) and activities that can be levelled easily (e.g., filling out a chart, identifying detail in a story, adding descriptive vocabulary) use stamps as quick assessment and motivation.
- Clearly level the stamps and share the levels with the students: for example, in a printing lesson, use the small stamp for some neat writing, the medium stamp for mostly neat work, and the large stamp for completely neat work.
- Give each student one pass. Tell them which stamp they will get and they can decide if they accept it or would like to try again.

Debrief

This kind of instant levelling works only on tasks that do not require creativity. They work well on skill-based activities or when students are incorporating a recently taught skill in their work. That said, stamps are a hit regardless of the age. Just be sure to get interesting ones.

Two Visits and Submit

- This routine is for work that can be marked on the spot.
- Explain the task: walk through the assignment or finish building the rubric.
- Explain that students can come to you twice for an evaluation while working. The third visit is an automatic acceptance of the mark.
- As students complete the task, they will come up and ask you what to do next. Offer the mark the work would receive at that time and the reason why; e.g., "This detail is a level 2 on the rubric."
- Students can decide if they are content with the mark given, or if they would like to work for a higher mark. (Students usually keep going.)
- Students can go back to the rubric to review the relevant section and what is required for a higher mark.
- Students know that they get only two evaluations prior to a final submission. This forces them to think about their work and review it carefully before coming to you for an evaluation.

Debrief

This instant feedback and forced review process can affect the class as a whole. I find that students are very careful about using their evaluations and do not waste them. They also end up listening very attentively to all the feedback offered to others. Often, a student will approach to another and say, "The teacher said you needed more detail. Can I see your story so I know if mine needs detail too?"

Natural Progression

- When students are creating a piece of work, allow for extra copies, in case a student wants to start over or fix something.
- Be mindful of your need to fix reversed letters or spelling mistakes. Provide examples around the room and give students a chance to explore each other's work, but hold back from correcting instantly. Allow students the opportunity to find the mistake and correct it themselves.

Debrief

This routine might reflect a philosophy more than just act as an activity, but doesn't every belief have its practice? The big idea is that we know what evolves naturally and what needs more specific instruction. Letting go of the constant need for the perfect bulletin board or publishing-ready work releases the tension caused in our students by the belief that they need to be perfect and that they cannot make mistakes. It is okay, and encouraged, for them to make mistakes and learn.

Make It Meaningful

- Post the objective somewhere visible, such as the chalkboard or interactive whiteboard.
- Circulate during the task.
- As you circulate, offer students a quick "You are showing _____ well" or a "You need to also show…" to reinforce their strengths and provide the next step in a specific and timely way.

Debrief

For feedback to be effective, it needs to be timely, useful, and appropriate. We need to provide it while students are still working on the task. Our feedback needs to address the expectation, what part they are demonstrating, and where to further expand. Our feedback can be written or verbal, but it needs to be current to be effective.

Routines for Self-Assessment

Student self-assessment provides insight into students' ability to independently reflect on their work and learning. It also helps develop critical and reflective thinkers in our classrooms. Encouraging self-assessment in our students must be scaffolded with clear modelling and guidelines. It must reflect each student's temperament and give insight into his/her skills. Asking students to simply provide a thumbs-up or thumbs-down as self-assessment is a great way to get a feel for the general class understanding, but it is a superficial reflection of an individual student's perception and ability. Having established routines around self-assessment can be beneficial, as it becomes a regular part of the learning process.

Personalized Checklists

Objectives:
For students to create checklists for editing their written work.
Key Words: resilience, self-regulation, individual
Suggested Grades: Junior/Middle

- After modelling how to edit one's work using a class checklist, encourage students to notice trends in their own written work. They can use the checklist, coupled with feedback from prior assessments and writing samples.
- Students create their own editing checklists for their written work. They might focus on bigger concepts (e.g., run-on sentences) or words that they commonly misspell.
- These checklists can also be used in peer editing.
- Every month or so, revisit the personalized checklists to see if there are new areas of focus.

Debrief

For this routine to be successful, students need to have a clear understanding of how to edit a piece of writing and how to correct the errors they find. For younger students, checklists might include only misspelled words. For older students, checklists will likely include bigger ideas, like looking for run-on sentences or using apostrophes correctly. Using personalized checklists gets students to home in on their trouble spots and improve their writing.

Take Three

Objective:
Encouraging students to do a careful review of content-based tests prior to submitting them.
Key Word: reflection
Suggested Grades: Junior/Middle

- When students are done writing a test, ask them to Take Three:
First Take: Read through the test and circle all the questions they answered but were unsure of.
Second Take: Read through the test a second time and look for numbers or words that are hastily written or not filled in completely.
Third Take: Read through the test a third time and make sure that the answers are correct and/or really show understanding and include examples.

- For each round of reviewing, students add a large check to the front of the test. Once students complete three takes, the test is handed in.

Debrief

You cannot stop the speedsters in your class, but Take Three helps slow students down. It also gives you rich assessment information about where they are unsure. I use Questions, Corrections, and Details to help my students remember what the Take Three stands for. I also post a visual poster of these steps at the front of the classroom during our tests.

Sticky-Note Goal-Setting

Objective:
To encourage students to set individual goals for their independent work.
Key Words: self-regulation, motivation
Suggested Grades: Primary/Junior/ Middle

- As a class, brainstorm a list of habits that are important in independent work. Ideas might include *asking questions when I don't understand something; staying focused on my own work; following instructions; writing neatly; getting details from the text; checking if my work is correct; getting materials independently.*
- You might have a general list to which you add specific ideas that are dependent on the type of independent work being done.
- Each student or group writes a goal on a sticky note. Reiterate what differentiates a *goal* and a *strength* to help students choose areas to work on.
- Place the sticky note near the workspace.
- As students work independently, stop during the work time and ask them to check in with themselves. Are they achieving their goal? If so, add a star to the sticky note.
- At the end of the task, ask students to attach their sticky-notes to their work.

Debrief

Sometimes the best kind of goal-setting is quick and has readily achievable results. My students love using this sticky-note system because it is an immediate reminder of what they want to work on. I also use sticky notes to redirect students who might not be reaching their goals during our work time. Sticky-note goals are ideal spots to record ideas from individual conferencing. Students can bring the notes back to their desk, check off goals as they complete them, and attach the sticky to their task when they submit it.

A Stuffy Moment

Objective:
To provide students with a space to read work aloud.
Key Words: resilience, independence
Suggested Grades: Early Primary/ Primary

- Provide each student with a stuffed animal or other interesting object.
- Explain that students will need to read their work aloud to their stuffies.
- Ask them to find a space in the room, hallway, or somewhere fairly isolated to begin.
- As they read, encourage them to edit and revise their work.

Debrief

By adding the element of an audience, despite its lack of life, the task of reviewing work becomes a bit more interesting. In writing pieces that are stuck in a spot or at the final stage, a quick read-aloud can re-energize the mood.

Collaborative Rubric

Objective:

To collaboratively create a rubric for assessment.

Key Words: assessment, critical thinking, student-driven

Suggested Grades: Primary/Junior/ Middle

- Create a large chart on the board.
- In the left column, outline the key areas to be assessed.
- Discuss what the area being assessed would look like as a level 4 (or A, the highest level), level 3, level 2, and level 1.
- Continue to list the areas of focus.
- Fill out a level 4 for each area, and then let students begin work.

Sample Rubric				
Area of Focus	Level 4	Level 3	Level 2	Level 1
Grasped the big idea				

Debrief

Collaborative rubrics really help students determine what they are being assessed on for a task. They enable and empower students. That said, students need to fill out only the areas of focus and level 4 criteria prior to moving on. Collaboratively filling in each box, as a whole lesson, can suck the excitement right out of the assignment. If you create the rubric on digital technology, such as Google Docs, the students can build it collaboratively and add to it as the assignment develops.

Routines for Peer Feedback

Peer feedback is an effective way of providing our students a chance to reflect, a chance to hear someone else's take on the assignment, and a chance to gather new strategies for improvement. Peer feedback also provides students with a chance to see perspective and practice empathy, as they find a way to share constructive feedback in a meaningful way.

High Five and Think About

Objective:

To give a framework for meaningful peer feedback.

Key Words: assessment, reflection

Suggested Grades: Early Primary/ Primary/Junior/Middle

- Review the concepts of *high five* (a strength) and *think about* (a goal for improvement). Reinforce that these comments are not accolades or put-downs; they are targeted comments reflective of the work itself.
- Ask students to share their work with a peer. Ideally, you have a rubric or some kind of assessment checklist that students can refer to.
- Each student gives one *high five* and one *think about* to the peer.

Debrief

Peer assessment needs to be focused and meaningful. The ideas of *high five* and *think about* are easy for students to grasp, and they allow them a way to talk about their peers' work.

Rubric Reflection

Objective:

To provide students, peers, and teachers a means of assessing the assignment.

Key Words: critical thinking, reflection

Suggested Grades: Primary/Junior/Middle

- Photocopy the class-created rubric on both sides of a piece of paper
- Have each student do a self-reflection on his/her assignment. They can use a specific color of pencil or highlighter to track the level they think they have achieved.
- Have students exchange the rubric and task with a peer. Have the peer complete the rubric on the other side of the paper.
- Have students use this feedback to go back and work on polishing their piece.

Debrief

Using the class-generated rubric, our students are all assessing using the same criteria. They know the expectations and have an understanding of what the objective is.

Peer Revise

Objective:

To encourage peer editing and feedback on a piece of writing.

Key Words: community-building, reflection

Suggested Grades: Primary/Junior/Middle

- Share the criteria for the writing piece with students.
- Talk about the difference between editing (looking for writing conventions) and revising (offering ideas and suggestions about the writing piece).
- Have students edit their own work, either online or using a colored pen on a hard copy.
- Have peers give feedback about the content of the writing piece. Many word processing programs offer a Comment function students can use. Or simply get revisers to use different-colored pens on hard copy.
- After reading and sharing, students revise their work according to the suggestions.

Debrief

I find that my students can catch errors in their writing conventions, but are not always able to identify when their written work is unclear or lacking detail. Having a peer revise their work gives them a second eye on their writing. Having peer revisers use the Comment function or a different-colored pen allows me to see the suggestions that students are giving one another.

Assessment *of* Learning

Assessment of learning takes place at the completion of the task or learning objective. It is the final stage. That said, learning is ongoing and builds. The reflective part of this process feeds into future activities and learning.

In this dialogue, teachers ask

- Did you meet your criteria?
- How do you feel about the task?
- Do you feel you addressed the big idea?
- What are the takeaways from this task that can help in future learning?
- What are the next steps for the student?

In this dialogue, students ask

- Did I meet the objectives or big idea for this topic?
- What knowledge did I gain?
- How will this knowledge influence my actions?

Routines for Quick Check-ins

Assessment does not have to be a formal process. Often we just need to know if our students understand the concept so that we can move on. It does not indicate that it is the end of the unit, or that the concept will not be reviewed again, but we need to know how comfortable the class feels prior to taking the next step. These routines are to help quickly gather a sense of who gets it and who needs more help.

Exit Pass

Objective:
To monitor students' take-aways from a lesson.
Key Words: reflection, independence, curiosity
Suggested Grades: Early Primary/ Primary/Junior/Middle

- When an activity is over and students are transitioning, consider using an Exit Pass, a response to a prompt or a sample of work from the activity. For example, in math, an exit pass might sound like this: *Before you meet me on the carpet for our book club, tell me a multiple of four* or *Before you head out to recess, please hand in your workbook as you leave the classroom.*
- For exit passes to be successful, teacher location is essential. The door works best for a transitional time when students are leaving the classroom.

Debrief

This is another simple strategy, but the words "Exit Pass" alert students to a few things: we are about to transition to a new activity; and we need to revisit what we've learned this class. It also is a very quick way to get a read on how an activity or lesson has gone. Just be mindful that the Exit Pass is quick—no teacher wants to hold up a line of wiggly and excited students.

Hand Continuum

Objective:
To gain perspective on how students feel about a concept.
Key Words: reflection, independence
Suggested Grades: Early Primary/ Primary/Junior/Middle

- Ask students to put their hands on their desks. Explain that this is the bottom of the continuum; it means "I do not understand one part of this concept." Explain that hands in the air means, "I completely get the concept."
- Ask students to place their hands somewhere on the continuum to show how much they understand the concept.

Debrief

This routine allows for a very quick assessment. From this, you can quickly make groups of who to help and who to extend. You can also buddy up those who need assistance. When going through a multi-step lesson, this check-in provides you with the information you need to guide the pace of the activity.

Visiting Alien

- Inform students that you have transformed into an alien. Explain that on your planet you have never heard of _____ (insert concept that you are assessing).
- Rotate around the room for a quick check-in: Can the student explain the concept? To what level? Do they just understand it; can they teach it to me; have they mastered it?

Debrief

This assessment routine is ideal when quickly assessing a few students you are wondering about. If you choose to rotate through the whole class, then this routine would no longer fit in the quick assessment category.

Muddiest Point

- As part of the lesson prep, post a list of the concepts that will be covered.
- When the lesson is complete, have students put a check beside the concept they thought was the muddiest. "Muddy" can mean difficult to understand, confusing, or challenging.

Debrief

Use this data to plan for the next lesson. What needs to be reviewed? What was the muddiest part? How could it be approached differently to help the students who struggled? Are there enough checks to review the concept as a whole class, make small groups, or use peer support?

Quick Focus

This routine was shared by teacher Michael Bushy.

- Prior to beginning teaching a new concept, give a very quick assessment of the last concept learned.
- The assessment is a written task, three or four questions focusing only on the last concept.
- Use data from this assessment to determine the next step.

Debrief

This strategy for checking in is very helpful when teaching material that scaffolds, such as math concepts. A quick check-in provides the essence of who has it, who needs review, and if the class is ready to move on to the next topic.

Objective:
To gain perspective on how students feel about a concept.
Key Words: independence, assessment
Suggested Grades: Early Primary/Primary/Junior

Objective:
For students to identify the most difficult part of the lesson.
Key Words: reflection, critical thinking
Suggested Grades: Junior/Middle

Objective:
To quickly assess one skill before moving on.
Key Words: assessment, independence
Suggested Grades: Primary/Junior/Middle

Routines for Assessing Bigger Projects

When assigning a larger task, one that will require more steps, we can use routines to help our students succeed.

Big Project Ideas

- dramatic productions
- monologues
- posters for a purpose
- models
- multimedia

- artwork
- booklets
- charting
- songs and poems

Step by Step

Objective:
To help students track their progress in projects.
Key Words: self-regulation, community-building
Suggested Grades: Early Primary/ Primary/Junior/Middle

- As a group, outline or review the tasks needed to complete the project. Record these steps on a long piece of chart paper.
- Provide each student with a clothespin or adhesive tag.
- Have each student record his/her name on the pin or tag and place it on the first step.
- Explain that, as students progress through the steps, they need to move their names.

Debrief

This quick chart helps anchor students in the process of the activity. It also allows them to see who is ahead of them, in case they need a question answered, or who is behind them, so they can offer support.

As-We-See-It Project Tracker

Objective:
To keep track of how students are progressing.
Key Words: reflection, resilience
Suggested Grades: Junior/Middle

- Keep a class list with the names of the students and the parts of the project. Put the chart in a collaborative or accessible space.
- Explain to students that this chart is where you are tracking their progress during the project.
- Model a few comments that you would include, such as
    X struggled with the first step, but asked a peer and moved quickly after.
    X is going quickly, but not reflecting.
    X is curious about _____ and finding the solution.
    X is very focused on editing and using the anchor chart to help.
- Add comments to the chart, but also encourage students to add comments under their own names to reflect on their learning.

Debrief

By the end of the project, this chart will become more valuable than the summative rubric. It will be an ongoing document of the journey of each student's learning. Sharing the document publicly lets students feel a part of their learning, as they see how we view their involvement and feel that they can also add their voice.

Routines for Documenting Student Information

There are formal processes in school boards and individual schools for documenting and sharing information about students; student records, internal portfolios, and report cards are created for organizing such information. But these formal documents represent only the summit of a mountain of information we have gleaned during the year. Having routines to help gather and organize information about our students helps make those times we create formal documents easier and more authentic.

Anecdotal Checklists

Objective:
To quickly assess students' social and organizational skills.
Key Words: assessment, reflection
Suggested Grades: Early Primary/ Primary/Junior/Middle

- Every month, identify four or five organizational skills or social skills to spotlight (usually ones being focused on at that time).
- Using a class list, create a checklist with those skills heading columns and students' names to head rows.
- Create your own checkmark system: e.g., one check for "moving toward," two checks for "established," and three checks for "strength."
- Put the checklist in a visible place near your work area. At a set time each day, grab the checklist and quickly evaluate one skill or focus for a few students at a time.
- Commit to trying to evaluate every student at least three times a month.

Debrief

When it comes to evaluating social-emotional or organizational skills on a report, I used to find that I was just going by memory or my perceived knowledge of a student. Using an anecdotal checklist proved beneficial: it showed me patterns in individual students and in the class; it helped me provide more authentic feedback to both parents and students around social and organizational skills; and it helped me establish what skills I wanted to work on with my students.

Collecting Assessment Information

Objective:
To gather assessment information on an ongoing basis in a manner that supports writing formal reports.
Key Words: academic, assessment
Suggested Grades: Early Primary/ Primary/Junior/Middle

- Either electronically or by hand, write the curriculum expectations of a specific learning objective for the term on a student mark sheet; e.g., *Reads numbers in the thousands, Compares and orders whole numbers.*
- When reviewing a piece of student work, use a check system or some other qualifier (e.g., levels 1, 2, 3, 4) to indicate how the student is reaching the expectation.
- In the evaluations, be clear if the assessment piece is formative or summative by highlighting or labelling.

Debrief

During report-card season, I used to be hunched over my desk, frantically decoding my scribbly anecdotes, reviewing a pile of stories to find out if students are consistently using capitals. Now I am laughing gleefully as I quickly reference students' assessment information. Okay, I am not laughing and there is no glee, but recording my assessment information according to curricular expectations can save much time and angst when writing reports.

Surveying Students

Objective:
To gather feedback from students on their thoughts about their work and the classroom learning environment.
Key Words: community-building, assessment, reflection
Suggested Grades: Primary/Junior/Middle

- Create an age-appropriate survey for your students. For older children, the survey might be multiple-choice with written responses. For younger children, the survey might have students color in a symbol to respond to statements.
- Your survey can target questions around learning styles, organizational skills, thoughts about a subject, or thoughts about instructional styles.
- Every term, or more often, have students complete a survey. There are many online options for surveys (Survey Monkey and Google Forms are two that I have used successfully) for which results are gathered and displayed for you.
- Use the surveys to help guide your teaching practice and offer insight into students' self-perception of their learning.

Debrief

I find student input very powerful when I am gathering information about my class. At times, their perception is very different from what I observe in class, and the surveys offer a conversation starter about those discrepancies. As well, surveys are useful for helping talk with parents, as I am offering not just my observations and opinions, but also sharing their own child's thoughts.

Tallying Up the Test

Objective:
Tracking additional information during a final test to determine next steps for a student.
Key Words: feedback, academic, goal-setting
Suggested Grades: Primary/Junior/Middle

- While students are quietly taking a test or completing an independent assignment, keep a pen close at hand.
- If a student asks you a question, place a tally mark beside the question.
- As students submit their work, keep it in the order the papers are handed in. You can also write the time it took to complete on the top corner of the paper.

Debrief

These subtle markings on the test or assessment can provide rich information to inform your marking. If a question has several tally marks and is correct, you will remember that the student struggled to understand it. If every question has one tally mark, it tells you that the student struggled to read the questions, but knew how to complete the task when it was read aloud. If a test is submitted in a short time frame with many errors, you have documentation of students who are not checking their work. If the task is submitted quickly with no errors, that student needs a challenge. If the test took a long time and has no errors, you most likely have a student that checks his/her work or is very careful. The extra markings and timing of text completion offer valuable insight beyond just a right/wrong assessment to help determine goals and next steps for each student.

Sample Test Analysis

This is a blog post I put on the class website for my Grade 5 students. When I taught Grade 1, I shared this information with the parents.

Dear Students:
I am super proud of all of you on your first math test! The results were wonderful. This means that you tried, made mistakes, learned and over all worked hard to understand these concepts.

As you move forward in math, I want you to think about the following:

1. How did you feel going into the math test?
2. How did you feel coming out of the test?

Think about the conversation we had about attitude and confidence in testing (do you remember the research on how your attitude affects your results?)

3. Look at your mark, sure. But also look at the pen markings. Remember that each time you asked a question, I put a small pen marking on the question. Even if you solved it in the end, go forward knowing that you need to review that concept. One pen mark usually means you just needed the question reread.

4. Compare your results to the order you handed it in (look at the number on the top of the page: 1 would be first and 19 was last). Did you hand in your test early and then have several mistakes? If so, you need to review your work more carefully. Did you hand it in quickly and still do well? If so, you need to visit Siberia more often. Did you hand in your test later and still have many errors? If so, you need to review the concepts and practice your basic facts.

The way I mark tests will always be similar, so you may want to save this as a reference.

Please remember that learning never ends, and we will use the knowledge from this unit to build into other math skills. You will have a chance to practice this learning again.

Take care.

Your Teacher

Color Recording

Objective:
To provide students with a space to record their prior knowledge and what they learned.
Key Words: assessment, independence, reflection
Suggested Grades: Early Primary/ Primary/Junior/Middle

- At the beginning of the unit, have students complete an assignment on concepts they will learn later. Ensure that they complete it in one color.
- Use this data for your formative assessment and to guide your teaching.
- Once the information has been obtained, have students go back to the same task and complete it in another color.
- If students find what they wrote is correct, they leave it, but they can correct mistakes and add information where they now perceive gaps.

Debrief

This assignment becomes a very effective tool for students to use to reflect on their learning. They can visually see what misconceptions they had and how much they have learned.

CHAPTER 7

Ending the School Day

Just as we start the day building our students for success, we end the day transitioning them to home as successfully as we can. Our end of the day is filled with expectations:

- Our classroom will be restored to some level of order.
- Our students will have the tools and instructions needed to complete any tasks at home.
- Our students will be packed and ready to leave our care.
- Our next day's plan will be lying in wait.

Typically, we leave the last part of the day—20 minutes to a half-hour—for closure. At the start of this time, we go over the homework for the evening. We refer to any ongoing projects, have students sort their belongings and supplies for the evening, and then have them find a book to read. When we buffer the end of the day with reading time, students who need more time to organize are provided it, and we get a chance to check with each student to ensure they are all organized, confident with their homework, and ready to go.

Routines for Cleaning Up

"Cleaning up the classroom" is a phrase that makes the task sound quite a bit more calm and relaxing than it is. This is the moment when we engage 30 children to complete the same task. Our usual fractioning applies: 1/4 are totally into it; 1/4 are not at all engaged, and 1/2 are on the fence, watching the tide and following the flow that seems most fun—which you hope is cleaning up. You might find that the second you start to clean up the room with students (or children), they seem to slow down or come to a complete halt, and cleaning becomes a solo show with you as the star. These routines are intended to empower students to take ownership of their materials.

Team-Building Class Clean-Up

Objective:
To empower and unite students while they clean the room.
Key Words: motivation, community-building
Suggested Grades: Early Primary/ Primary/Junior

- Find a way to track the time: posting on the wall, counting out loud, using a digital stopwatch on the interactive whiteboard, etc.
- At the end of an activity, challenge students to clean up the room—to guest-ready condition—as fast as they can.
- Explain that students will need to work as a team and all must participate. You won't need to overstress this, as they will work harder for the team then they would for a teacher.

- Negotiate a reasonable time and challenge them to beat it.
- Walk out of the classroom and shut the door. Promise that you will not look or peek in—and keep that promise. If your students are younger, you might want to pop in every so often (with your eyes shut, of course) and let them know how much time is left.
- Instruct students to yell, "Ready!" when they are done. Then you can go in and stop the timer.

Debrief

This activity can get tired if used every day for each lesson. I pull it out only after very messy inquiry lessons; i.e., about twice a week. You might find it useful to debrief the clean up, to ask if there was anything that worked well or anything that needs improvement. Often the fact that one or two students do not help causes frustration to others. This can prompt an excellent conversation about working as a team. For fun, play a song and challenge students to clean up before the song is finished. For a competitive class, post the time of the last clean-up as the record to beat.

Mystery Item Clean-Up Challenge

Objective:
To motivate students to clean up the classroom.
Key Word: motivation
Suggested Grades: Early Primary/ Primary/Junior

- Let students that know there is a mystery item that needs to be put away. To ensure honesty, write down the mystery item before starting.
- Explain that, as they clean up, you will be keeping an eye on this item. If the item is put away, that student will receive an award. Use some sort of extrinsic motivation as the award: e.g., a cheer, a symbolic toy or object the winner can keep on his/her desk for the day.

Debrief

This activity provides a bit of mystery and challenge to students who need to be motivated to clean up. If you can manage to keep the air of suspense, you might not need to write down the item.

Alphabet Clean-Up

Objective:
To encourage classroom clean- up while embedding critical thinking.
Key Words: motivation, academic, critical thinking
Suggested Grades: Early Primary/ Primary

- Break students into groups. Assign each group a series of letters from the alphabet: i.e., Group 1, a–f; Group 2, g–l; Group 3, m–r; Group 4, s–z.
- Explain that students need to put away objects that begin with a letter from their group.
- To keep the groups moving and to keep them from renaming objects so they can leave them, provide a space where groups can tally how many objects they have picked up.
- You can even be more specific and create tally chart for each letter of the alphabet.
- Use this data to discuss common letters: *What letters do most objects start with? Why are there no X words?*

Debrief

This activity can easily be extended to a look at three-dimensional objects. The shape conversation nicely leads into discussion about why the cylinder is the most commonly misplaced shape (my kids are always dropping pencils and markers) and about strategies to solve that problem. Other variations include

- Cleaning up by color
- Cleaning up by size of object; incorporating measurement
- Assigning each piece you pick up an adjective; remember your best adjective and the class will guess the object it matches
- Cleaning up by type of simple machine
- Cleaning up by type of material the object is made from

Area Managers

Objective:
To assign one student responsibility for each area of the room.
Key Words: self-regulation, student-driven
Suggested Grades: Early Primary/Primary/Junior/Middle

- Divide the room into equal sections. You can divide based on how many students you have or put students into groups and divide based on the number of groups.
- Using a simple matching method, assign each area of the room to a student or group.
- If you are using groups, let students know that you need a manager for each group, someone to be ultimately responsible. They can apply to you directly with a short note.

Debrief

This routine works best if the groups rotate areas regularly. Some areas are typically cleaner than others, and rotating lets all students have an equal chance to prove themselves. If you decide to choose managers, rotating this position also gives each student the chance to lead the pack.

Desk Management

Objective:
To empower students to manage the cleanliness of their desks.
Key Words: motivation, independence
Suggested Grades: Primary/Junior/Middle

- Create a ticket, card, or sticker that can be proudly displayed. Write *Never to Be Checked Again* on it.
- Routinely check the tidiness of the desks. If a student keeps his/her desk in perfect order, track it.
- After five checks, a student whose desk has always been clean and tidy earns the *Never to Be Checked Again* marker. The sticker can be proudly displayed and serves as a reminder that you never need to check that desk again.

Debrief

Creating a rubric for a clean desk (using pictures or words) will help struggling students visualize what is expected. Students should also be aware that a *Never to Be Checked Again* sign can be revoked if the student starts to model lower levels of organization or if objects are lost in the desk.

Routines for Getting Out the Door

How do we leave the classroom in a way that is meaningful and calm? Common sense would dictate that thirty bodies can not go through a door frame at the same time but, as we know from watching students go to recess, common sense does not always prevail. So we need established routines around dismissing students and getting them ready to move calmly and quietly through the school.

Line Up

Objective:

To ensure you have all your students prior to leaving the classroom.

Key Words: independence, community-building

Suggested Grades: Early Primary/ Primary/Junior

- At the sound of a noisemaker (or bell), students arrange themselves in order from tallest to smallest, or in alphabetic order by first name or last name, or in order of birthday months.
- Tell students if the lining up needs to be done silently or with talking.
- Once students are in the line-up, ask them who is missing from their line.

Debrief

You can challenge students to think of other ways to line up and sort themselves into groups.

Work Collection

Objective:

To check to see who has handed in class work or homework.

Key Words: self-regulation, motivation

Suggested Grades: Early Primary/ Primary/Junior/Middle

- Take the pile of class work or homework to the door. (I carry a check slip with all the students' names on it.)
- Call out the names on the work you are holding. Those students leave the classroom.
- Once you have called out the names of those students who have handed in their work, talk with any remaining students about where their work is.

Debrief

This is simple and it works. I have found this routine to be very helpful for students who need organizational support, as it combines a verbal and visual reminder about what needs to be handed in. Also, it helps nudge repeat "no name" offenders to put their names on their work.

At the end of each day, I put magnet cards on the B.I.N., or Books I Need, board and students know what books to take home. The cards are color-coded by subject.

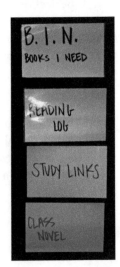

The Flop

Objective:
To provide students with a quiet moment before they leave the classroom.
Key Words: independence, motivation, reflection
Suggested Grades: Early Primary/ Primary/Junior

- At the end of a class or a change of activity, give an established signal for the Flop.
- At the signal, students flop onto a space on the floor. You will want to practice this beforehand; offer suggestions about how to flop and where a suitable quiet space is.
- Turn off the lights.
- After a minute or so, turn on the lights, and students must move silently and calmly into line.

Debrief

We do this routine as a game. The students beg to flop. The follow-up movement of travelling silently to line encourages them to continue to be mindful of their personal space and others.

Ninja Line

Objective:
To silently form a line.
Key Words: motivation, self-regulation
Suggested Grades: Early Primary/ Primary/Junior

- Have a class discussion around how a ninja, or anyone stealthy, moves.
- Choose one student in the class to be the watch guard. This student closes his/her eyes or is blindfolded; he/she is spun in a few circles at the centre of the classroom.
- On your silent signal, students must travel to where they will line up without making any noise.
- The student on watch will point in the direction of any sound. Any students caught making sound must return to their seats and try again.
- Once the majority of the students have made it to the line, ask all students to travel to the line.

Debrief

When we have time for it, this line-up routine is a class favorite. Students love the game element and the excitement of catching out others making sound. I love the silence. I used to offer incentives to be quiet for this line-up routine, but have realized that lining up "ninja style" is incentive enough. We also like to travel through the halls like ninjas—I challenge students to not be seen by anyone inside another classroom.

Student Reflection

Objective:
To give students a chance to reflect on their choices that day.
Key Words: reflection, self-regulation
Suggested Grades: Early Primary/ Primary/Junior/Middle

This activity was shared by teacher Michael Bushy.

- Create a chart with key words for character traits that you are working on as a class, attributes you are focusing on. Examples of key words include

responsible	caring
respectful	responsible
focused	on-task
unsettled	distracted
unorganized	poor choices
awesome	

- Ensure that the list of words is limited to a few and include a variety of positive and negative traits.
- Post the chart on the door. As your students walk out, have them quickly touch the word that describes the choices they made that day.

Debrief

This is a great way for students to really reflect on their choices at the end of the day. As an alternative to touching the chart, students can fill out a Choice Continuum. Regardless of what you ask, remember that what is important is that each student reflects and provides a quick example.

Sample Choice Continuum

Today, I made _____ choices.

Positive ——————————————————————————— Negative

CHAPTER 8

Routines Beyond the Classroom

Every classroom is a microcosm of the bigger world. We strive to create a warm, caring, productive, engaging, and dynamic environment. We want our students to feel secure, comfortable taking risks, and empowered in our classroom. And then we open the doors.

Outside of our classrooms, there are different influences that affect our world: other teachers, students, parents, administrators, and guests from the community. Just as we need to create clear routines to help the world of our classroom function, we need routines to establish guidelines and expectations for interacting with others beyond that classroom door.

What do we consider when we are building routines outside of the classroom?

School Culture: Just as we have routines within our classroom, a school establishes its own routines around home–school communication, relationships within the community, technology guidelines, health and safety practices, student behavior, and environmental issues…to name a few. Some of these routines are mandated by a school board, while others have been created by school administration. Ideally, these routines work to support your classroom community.

Parent Community: The parent community can greatly shape the dynamic in our classrooms and our schools. In some schools, it is a struggle to build a bridge to the parent population; in others, it is a struggle to keep parents from overwhelming teachers with their needs and demands. Having clear routines around parent involvement can help create a balance or a bridge.

Colleagues and Other Students: For understanding how to appreciate others, form relationships, and respect the people around us, interacting with the other "regular" people at our school is vital for our students. We need them to feel connected to our school and the people in the school community.

We want the security and value that we create in our students to transcend our classroom walls. In a similar vein, the way we, as educators, interact with our colleagues and students' parents also reflects our class community.

Routines for Home Communication

As teachers, we spend more waking hours during weekdays with our students than many parents spend with their own children. If parents work outside the home, they likely have even less time with their children in the mornings and evenings. And speaking as a working parent myself, the value of having established routines for communicating with parents is paramount in establishing a trusting and informed relationship between home and school.

When building routines for sharing information with parents, it is important to ask the following questions.

What information do parents need to know?

- Parents need to know specific information related to their own child: when they are doing well, and when they need assistance.
- Parents often want a sense of what their child is currently learning in school. This gives them the opportunity to connect with the curriculum outside of the classroom.
- Parents want to know about your routines and your expectations.

How do I want to communicate with parents?

- If you need to contact a parent, will you phone? Use e-mail? Write a note? E-mail has the advantage of allowing you to create a paper trail, should you need one. A note home can be more personal. Making a phone call can be helpful when the issue might be misconstrued in writing; a parent might need to be able to ask questions as they hear about the issue.
- If you want to establish a regular line of communication with parents, consider how often you will contact them. Will it be a monthly letter home? An excerpt about your class in a schoolwide newsletter? Are you setting up a manageable expectation for yourself?

What is my goal in communicating with parents?

- Before you contact individual parents or the parents of an entire class, be clear on your goal. Are you looking to give them a snapshot of life in the classroom? Are you trying to get support for a student or group of students?

If I am asking for support from parents, is my request reasonable and timely?

- If you are asking for support from home, have a plan in place, including suggestions, before you contact the parents. Do not contact parents to raise an alarm if you do not have feedback for how you are working to support the issue in the classroom.
- Be realistic when asking for support.
- Timing is essential. Calling a parent to talk about a low mark a few days before the reports are sent home does not foster trust between home and school.

What's Happening in the Classroom?

Objective:
To inform families about what is happening in the classroom.
Key Words: academic, reflection
Suggested Grades: Early Primary/ Primary/Junior/Middle

- At the end of every month, work with students to brainstorm highlights from the month. Take this time to talk to your class about exciting things coming up.
- Ask students to write a letter (or send an e-mail or a voice thread) home, describing what is happening in class.

Debrief

Incorporating a writing sample for parents, as well as information about what is happening in the classroom, makes this routine multi-tasking genius. For younger children, you might write part of the letter, photocopy it, and allow them to add a few words.

QR Routines

- Create a QR code that can give parents a link to a PDF that contains your classroom routines.
- The linked document should contain information about routines that affect home: i.e., homework routines, classroom schedules, routines around formal assessment, and routines around home–school communication.
- You can also create a QR code to link to the classroom schedule or a list of other teachers for the class.
- Post the QR code in a visible spot by your door or send the QR code home at the start of the year.

Debrief

Most people are more inclined to scan a QR code than to read a lengthy description hanging by the classroom door. As the year progresses, change the QR codes or have students help modify the information outside the door.

Two Things

- Prior to contacting parents about a concern or a request, think of two meaningful ways they can support their child at home.
- Be realistic in what you are asking; consider resources and time constraints.
- Make your support ideas simple and manageable.

Debrief

It is important to contact parents when you are concerned about a student's progress or when you have a specific request. Share your classroom plan for support, but also offer explicit ways that support can be provided at home.

Responsible Problem-Solving

- If there is an incident at school, find an authentic way for the student to communicate the issue with parents.
- After debriefing with the student(s) involved, have them write a letter home or, if possible, call home to talk to their parents.

Objective:
To create a space where you can share information about classroom routines.
Key Words: community-building, independence
Suggested Grades: Early Primary/ Primary/Junior/Middle

Objective:
To target the support you ask from parents or guardians.
Key Word: community-building
Suggested Grades: Early Primary/ Primary/Junior/Middle

Objective:
Student communication with parents.
Key Words: student-driven, resilience
Suggested Grades: Early Primary/ Primary/Junior/Middle

Problem Discussion Sheet 1

Name: _____

DESCRIBE: What happened? Describe the issue and your actions.

LEARN: How can you make sure this problem does not happen again?

SHARE: Please talk to your parents about today's incident. They might have some ideas to add to the LEARN section.

_____

_____   _____

Signed (by you and your teacher)   Date

Parent(s) signature: _____

Pembroke Publishers ©2015 *Classroom Routines for Real Learning* by Jennifer Harper and Kathryn O'Brien ISBN 978-1-55138-297-5

Problem Discussion Sheet 2

Name: _____

SHARE: Write (or draw) what happened. Describe your actions.

LEARN: Write (or draw) what you could do differently.

SHARE: Please talk to your parents about today's incident. They might have some ideas to add to the LEARN section.

_____

_____   _____

Signed (by you and your teacher)   Date

Parent(s) signature: _____

Pembroke Publishers ©2015 *Classroom Routines for Real Learning* by Jennifer Harper and Kathryn O'Brien ISBN 978-1-55138-297-5

- In their communication with their parents, students should describe the incident, their role in the incident, and the plan for moving forward.
- If a teacher (or parent) wishes to discuss the incident, they can do so in a follow-up phone call, meeting, or note.

Debrief

When students have had an incident at school, the easiest way to communicate with parents is for the teacher to contact the parents and describe the incident. However, in this cycle of communication, we have removed the child and lessened their responsibility for acknowledging their part in the incident and the solution. I always ask the child to fill out a reflection and send it home to share it with parents; see Problem Discussion Sheets on pages 108 and 109. The following day, depending on the nature of the incident, I might follow up by contacting the parents.

Routines for Sharing Student Work

Classrooms are hives of activity. There are so many incredible things going on in so many classrooms, how do we share the work of our students? If you have a bulletin board outside your classroom, you can display student work. You can also have students present their work at assemblies. But how can we share work on a more regular basis?

Learning Exchange

Objective:
To have students share their work with their peers at school.
Key Words: academic, community-building, motivation, student-driven
Suggested Grades: Early Primary/Primary/Junior/Middle

- At the end of a unit, or when your class has mastered a particular skill, hold a learning exchange with another class. A learning exchange is a 15- to 20-minute visit to another class to learn about a new skill or subject area.
- Learning exchanges are not presentations. They are interactive, small-group discussions through which your students teach the new skill or share a few facts with the other class.
- At the end of the learning exchange, you can give students a reflection slip where they can jot down their new learnings.

Debrief

My students love learning exchanges, and I purposely keep them very simple. We recently did one in which they shared their multiplication skill with an older class. They used chart paper and markers to help explain their ideas.

Teach-Someone-Else Slips

Objective:
For students to teach a new skill or concept to someone else.
Key Words: student-driven, academic, assessment, independence
Suggested Grades: Early Primary/Primary/Junior/Middle

- As a summative task, prepare a teach-someone-else slip for the skill. The slip could include a big idea and supporting details; it could be an example of a math concept; it could be a connection between a science concept and their daily life. It is a space to share a short summary of the learning.
- Students must take the slip home and find someone to teach the skill to.
- The parent "student" evaluates the student "teacher" on his/her ability to explain the new skill.

Debrief

This routine is similar to the Learning Exchange (page 110), but it is a more formal teaching activity, for which students are evaluated on their ability to explain the new skill to someone else.

Share This Folder

Objective:
To share work with home or other people in the school community.
Key Words: reflection, community-building
Suggested Grades: Early Primary/Primary/Junior/Middle

- At the beginning of the year, create a Share This folder for each student. Students can decorate it or individualize it in a way that makes it unique to them.
- At different points in the year, ask students to select a piece of work they want to share. This work can be shared with a person in the school community or someone at home.
- The student delivers the folder, with their chosen piece of work inside, to the individual, and spends a few minutes describing their work.
- The work is then returned to school in the Share This folder.

Debrief

Sharing work is not a special or new routine, but without the folder the work is too easily lost and often never appreciated as a proper "share." When they take the time to put the work in a personalized folder, students seem to take more pride in showing people what they have done. I also like using the folder to share singular pieces, rather than having people see many work samples at once.

Routines for Recess

While not a subject itself (although many of my students would argue to change that), recess is a time that is rich in opportunities for learning. It is an essential time for students to mix with a diverse group of peers and to practice developing their social skills. While there is an important element of natural problem-solving (or playground politics, as we used to call it) as children play together and negotiate their needs, they also need to practice clear routines to ensure their safety and social well-being.

Recess Expectations

Objective:
To establish clear guidelines for behavior during recess time.
Key Words: community-building, empathy
Suggested Grades: Early Primary/Primary/Junior/Middle

- Some schools have recess policies; I prefer to establish recess expectations as a class.
- Use student input to create a list of expectations. These expectations should include how to go outside for recess, how to include peers in play, how to deal with problems, and how to come in from recess. For students in the middle years, it might be the expectation that they need to go outside or wear a coat in weather hovering below 10°C.
- Post expectations in a clear spot in the classroom.
- At least once a month, revisit the expectations and modify them (especially during season changes).

Debrief

As part of attendance after recess, I will often ask my students to rate their recess according to our expectations.

What Can I Do?

Objective:
To encourage free play.
Key Word: independence,
Suggested Grades: Early Primary/
Primary/Junior/Middle

This photo shows a recess brainstorm we did on the first snow day. As the winter goes on, we revisit this list and add new ideas.

- Keep an ongoing list in your classroom about the games that are happening at recess.
- If a student is new or having difficulties socially, he/she can look at the list to have ideas of what games to play.

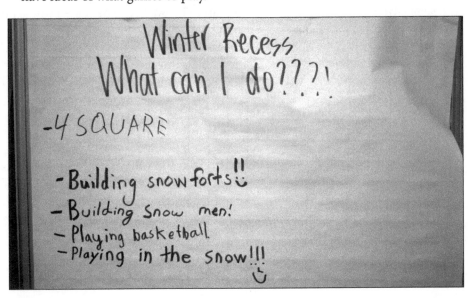

Debrief

While it might seem deflating to imagine that children need guidance to know how to play freely, some of them do. Having a list of potential games helps students who are struggling to join a peer group; it is also helpful to start conversations around what are safe activities at recess time. Some teachers I know have actually brought back recess games that were popular many years ago—hopscotch became a very competitive activity last spring at my friend's school.

In Defence of Recess

A Gallup poll conducted by the Robert Wood Johnson Foundation found that 77% of principals will withhold recess as a disciplinary measure. The study also revealed how often recess gets affected in the average school week. When a student needs extra support, when work is not getting done, when students are not behaving in class, when teachers are overloaded with curriculum to cover, when students are writing long standardized tests, recess is often the time that gets taken away. There has been considerable research done to show the importance of recess, not only as a time to develop personal relationships, but also as a time to rejuvenate and energize the brain. Students who lose recess on a daily basis actually show poorer academic performance than those who have a regular recess time. It's a simple equation. Recess = a happier, more engaged student.

Recess Buddies

Objective:
To help students work together through social issues.
Key Words: empathy, community-building
Suggested Grades: Early Primary/ Primary/Junior

- Identify a student that needs support during recess.
- Select a buddy you think will be able to help the struggling student.
- Bring the students together prior to the start of recess. Explain to both that you would appreciate if they could be buddies during the recess. They can play any games that fit in the recess rules, but you are asking that they stick together.
- Have the students come back and share the experience.

Debrief

Some students need a bit of a push at recess to engage in play. They might not understand the game, feel a part of the group, or understand how to respond in a social setting. A recess buddy helps build empathy and create a relationship. Recess Buddy could also be a rotating job on the job board: the Recess Buddy circulates to ensure everyone feels included.

Routines Around Absent Students

It is inevitable, especially once winter flu season begins, that students will be absent from school. Every teacher has his or her own policy around completing missed work. If students know the class routines around what to do when they have missed school, it helps lessen anxiety and ease their transition back into the classroom.

Away-for-a-Day Buddy

Objective:
To address the fact that an absent student misses both classwork and connecting with peers.
Key Words: motivation, peer support, risk-taking
Suggested Grades: Junior/Middle

- At the start of the year, group students in groups of three or four. Explain that the other students in the group are their Away-for-a-Day buddies.
- Older students can exchange phone numbers or e-mail addresses. Younger students can exchange names to be shared with adults at home.
- If a student is away for a day (or more), the peer group is responsible for calling or e-mailing the student, or keeping a short note about what happens during the school day.
- The purpose of this group is less to help the student know what they have missed academically than to help them continue to feel connected with peers socially.

Debrief

This activity takes some modelling. As a teacher, I have written short sticky notes to students absent with an illness and put them in their personal bins. This can be a risk-taking activity for older students who are encouraged to call or e-mail peers. If you have access to a phone in class, you can let the group call from school. This activity can be a positive reinforcement to those students who are away, reminding them of their connection to the classroom.

Day-of-the-Week Folders

Objective:
To provide a space where students can access information from previous days.
Key Words: self-regulation, independence
Suggested Grades: Junior/Middle

- Set up a system of magazine folders or file folders to match the days of the week, a rotational schedule (e.g., day 1 to 8 of a unit), or the subjects you teach.
- When you copy a class set of work, make a few extra copies. Place all extra sheets in the magazine folders.
- If students are away or lose a sheet, they know where to get one without asking you.

Debrief

This system is designed to enable and empower our students. They can seek out what they are missing without having to ask, "What sheets did I miss?"

> Teacher Lisa Chesworth writes the name of absent students on the sheets as they are handed out. This strategy prevents them from being lost and reminds others that a copy needs to be reserved for the absent student.

Routines for Trips

Field trips, as exciting as they are for students, require careful planning. Given that field trips are not part of our day-to-day activities, the routines around leaving the school are less practiced and therefore even more important. Most schools and school boards have clear policies and guidelines around planning and organizing a field trip. This section includes routines for preparing your students to go on a field trip as well as a few to practice while on the field trip.

Field Trip Scavenger Hunt

Objective:
To give students a focus while they are on their field trip.
Key Words: curiosity, independence
Suggested Grades: Early Primary/ Primary/Junior/Middle

- Prior to the field trip, tell students that they will be on a visual scavenger hunt; i.e., they will find the items by looking, not touching.
- Provide your students with three or four things to look for on the field trip. If you know the program, they could be specific facts or something they will see. If you don't know the program, it could be something related more generally to the purpose of the field trip; e.g., *Find one animal that hibernates* or *When the guide is sharing information, listen for one clue about how Greeks cleaned themselves.*
- On the way back to school, see who found everything on the list.

Debrief

My students love scavenger hunts, and I find the idea keeps them focused during presentations and tours.

Blob In!

Objective:
To get students to quickly move together in a group.
Key Word: motivation
Suggested Grades: Early Primary/ Primary/Junior

- When on a field trip, if you need the students' attention, call "Blob in!"
- At the sound of these code words, your students need to walk quickly to form a "blob" around your outstretched hand.
- Depending on the space, you can instruct your students that they must silently blob in.

Debrief

When travelling in the outside world, it is good to have a signal for the students to quickly huddle together, especially if you do not want to raise your voice outside or in an open space. My students love "blobbing" together, and it is a quick and easy routine to get them ready to listen or to transition to the next tip. We add extra dramatic effect by getting them to wobble on spot (without touching anyone) until everyone arrives.

Pack It Up

Objective:
To encourage students to be responsible for preparing for trips.
Key Words: resilience, self-regulation, independence
Suggested Grades: Primary/Junior/ Middle

- A few days before your field trip, talk to students about logistical items; e.g., What clothes do we need? Do you need a lunch? What activities will we be doing? Do you need water? Do you need sunscreen?
- From this conversation, discuss what students will need to enjoy their field trip or overnight trip.
- On a sticky note, have students write down the items they need for the trip. (For younger children, an adult can scribe and copy the list.) For overnight trips, you might want to prepare a master list as a class.
- Send the note home with the reminder that the students need to be prepared for the field trip. If appropriate for students' age, encourage them to get organized independently.

Debrief

I have had the pleasure of going on many overnight trips with my students. Within the first few minutes of getting to the destination, it becomes strikingly clear which students participated in packing their bags, and which students did not give the trip a second thought. Having a class conversation around getting prepared for the trip helps students actually think about what they need to bring and, occasionally, it inspires them to pack their gear on their own so they know how to find it.

Routines for Bringing in Guests

I use the word *guests* broadly to include student teachers, parent volunteers, supply teachers, presenters, and anyone else who is not part of our immediate school community. I love having visitors, and so do my students. The energy and the ideas of new people can invigorate the room. I have found that guests will observe different traits in my students from the ones I do, and see new dynamics in the classroom. But if students are not used to having guests and there are no routines around inviting and integrating guests into a classroom, having visitors can be disruptive.

Depending on the nature of the guest, students need to have the opportunity to meet the guest, to understand what their role is within the classroom, and to have a chance to develop a rapport with the guest. Guests who are visiting as presenters are likely very comfortable taking the lead with students and have their own routines to bring to your classroom.

If the guest is a student teacher, a supply teacher, or a volunteer, they might need guidance in how to integrate into the classroom. With these individuals, we need to have information available to explain how we frame our day, and what routines we use around behavior, independent work, and collaborative learning. This can happen in a meeting or through a folder of information. New ideas and suggestions are always welcome but, in the beginning, I ask visitors to follow our familiar routines while they get to know the students and myself. Small courtesies, like having name tags or nameplates for students as well as providing the visitor with a class list and schedule, help to make people feel welcome.

Who Are You?

Objective:
To get to know the individual visiting the classroom.
Key Words: curiosity, community-building
Suggested Grades: Early Primary/ Primary/Junior/Middle

- Ask a new visitor to bring in some objects that would describe them.
- In a comfortable setting, the visitor shares the objects with the class. Students guess information about the person.
- In turn, in small groups, students can meet the visitor and share one or two ideas of objects to represent themselves.

Debrief

There are many different icebreakers and "get to know you" games. I like this one because it is fairly calm and encourages great questions and inferences. If visitors don't have objects to bring, they could write down two or three facts about themselves (including one silly untrue fact) and students can guess which facts are true and which are false.

Greeters

Objective:

To encourage student greeters to talk to the visitor about classroom routines.

Key Words: community-building, student-driven

Suggested Grades: Early Primary/ Primary/Junior/Middle

- If you have greeters (students who greet newcomers) this routine is an obvious one for them. If not, you can appoint two or three students to act as "greeters" for the newcomer.
- The role of the greeters is to explain what the class is doing.
- The visitor should sit by the greeters and be prepared for a steady stream of information about the classroom.
- Greeters are like the broadcasters at a hockey game or the commentators on animal discovery shows—their role is to share observations about the classroom with the visitor.

Debrief

By pairing the visitor with greeters, you give the visitor the opportunity to learn about the class while developing a rapport with a few students right away. Have greeters take the visitor for a tour of the school, take them out for recess, show them where materials are in the classroom...and the greeters are always very keen to oblige!

Observational Checklists

Objective:

To encourage the visitor to observe individual students and/or teacher–student interactions.

Key Words: assessment, reflection

Suggested Grades: Early Primary/ Primary/Junior/Middle

- Give your visitor the names of one or two students to observe each day. Ask the visitor to look for certain social-emotional skills or organizational skills. Be clear that the visitor should not record the name of the students on the notes.
- If you are also in the classroom, you might ask the visitor to observe the class dynamic around certain routines: e.g., What do you notice during a transition time? When students were working in small groups, are they participating?
- Take the time to listen to the observations of the visitor.

Debrief

Having had many student teachers and supply teachers, I have found that asking them to perform a specific task helps provide direction. As well, their observations often encourage me to shift the spotlight as a new strength or area of concern might be noted. Supply teachers are incredibly busy during the day, but can give important insight about different students or a class's ability when you are not there.

We Thank You!

Objective:

To model how to thank someone who has visited the classroom.

Key Words: reflection, empathy, community-building

Suggested Grades: Early Primary/ Primary/Junior/Middle

- When a visitor has been to the classroom, consider an appropriate thank-you.
- For a presenter or supply teacher who has visited for a day, a thank-you might be two students making an announcement on behalf of the class. For a student teacher or long-term volunteer, a thank-you might be a book, a handwritten card or note, or a piece of artwork from the class.
- When encouraging your students to say "thank you," make sure they include explicit examples of what they are thankful for.

Debrief

My golden rule in the classroom is to give thanks. Building a sense of gratitude in our classroom is very important. Whenever we have a visitor or a volunteer on a field trip, or someone who has gone out of their way, we say thanks. My favorite way to thank student teachers is having my students write them reference letters; these are always wonderful testimonies to the impact the student teacher has had on our classroom learning.

Routines for Taking Action

How do we encourage our students to take authentic action outside of our classroom? There are a number of organizations that offer opportunities for students to take action, locally and globally. It is challenging to create routines around taking action, as often the action our students engage in are one-off events, like fundraisers or food drives. While these types of action projects are powerful learning experiences, they do not usually evolve into a sustainable routine for classroom. But if even one student per class truly connects to a class action project, they might modify their personal routines or become vocal advocates for a cause as part of an ongoing action in their own lives.

What Can We Do?

Objective:

To foster conversations around students taking action outside the classroom.

Key Words: empathy, student-driven, community-building

Suggested Grades: Early Primary/ Primary/Junior/Middle

- In class, as part of your conversations around current events (local and global), regularly ask your students, "What can we do?"
- Share different types of action with your students. These might include educating and informing others; political action (petitions, writing letters); consumer choices (considering what things are being bought); fundraisers; "Getting Dirty" projects (creating a green space, cleaning up a park); lifestyle choices (walking to school).
- When students are very interested and engaged in a current event, refer to the types of action and ask them, "What can we do?"
- Your class might decide to do a whole-class action in response to a current event or issue, or the conversation might spark the interest of a few students to independently act.

Debrief

Inspiring authentic student action needs to be scaffolded. When we extend our conversations about current events to discussions about action, many of my students become more mindful about what we, as individuals, can do and what our community is doing to create positive change.

Gratitude Spies

Objective:

To encourage students to find and recognize small acts of kindness in the school community.

Key Words: student-driven, empathy, motivation

Suggested Grades: Early Primary/ Primary/Junior/Middle

- Tell students that they will be spies on the look out for acts of kindness around the school.
- You might want to start within your classroom: a student secretly observes another student to look for a positive action, and then shares those observations in a class meeting.

- When your students "spy" something positive, they write a note (or you help them write a note) that they secretly deliver to the individual or group who performed the act of kindness.

> # Dear Ms. McCormack,
>
> # We are very thankful that you help us take risks to eat different vegetables and foods at lunch.
>
> # From, The Nice Ninjas

Debrief

My students will likely disown me for revealing this, our top spy secret. But it is such a positive routine, I had to share it. If you are a student or teacher at my school, please keep our secret! It fulfills the adage: to increase your own happiness, make someone else happy.

Gratitude in Action

We had a bit of a debate about including routines around gratitude as part of routines to create student action. Sociologist Georg Simmel called gratitude "the moral memory of mankind." Without it, our society would crumble. Gratitude serves to connect us in small, real, human ways. When students want to take action, it is often prompted by an understanding of something they are grateful for (like healthy food) that someone else does not have. Through taking the time to encourage gratitude among students, you are encouraging them to take action by being grateful for others and for what they have.

Gratitude Chains

Many thanks to Adrienne Fisher for contributing this idea.

Objective:
To develop a sense of gratitude within the school community.
Key Words: empathy, community-building
Suggested Grades: Early Primary/Primary/Junior/Middle

- Cut a large number of paper strips for a paper chain.
- Ask each student in the class to write one example of what they are grateful for on a strip.
- Use these gratitude strips to make a chain. Hang the chain in the classroom and encourage students to continue to add to the chain throughout the year.

Debrief

We created a gratitude chain as a whole school. After a few months, it had snaked its way from the second floor down to the basement. Any time I was feeling low, I took a look at the sentiments on the gratitude chain. Reading students' and teachers' words of thanks helped pick me up many times.

Bibliography

Artful Thinking. Accessed November 24, 2014. http://www.pzartfulthinking. org/index.php.

Bennett, Barrie Brent, and Noreen Carol Bennett (2001) *Beyond Monet: The Artful Science of Instructional Integration*. Toronto, ON: Bookation.

Cheney, C.O. (1989) "Preventive Discipline through Effective Classroom Management" Paper presented at the Preconvention Training Program "Exploring the Theory/Practice Link in Special Education" at the Annual Convention of the Council for Exceptional Children. ERIC Document Reproduction Service No. ED 304 869.

Connolly, John (2006) *The Book of Lost Things*. New York, NY: Atria Books.

Covino, Eric, and Edward Iwanicki (1996). "Experience Teachers: Their Constructs of Effective Teaching" *Journal of Personnel Evaluation in Education* 10: 325–63.

Dewey, John (1916) *Democracy and Education*. New York, NY: Macmillan Company.

Duhigg, Charles (2012) *The Power of Habit: Why We Do What We Do in Life and Business*. New York, NY: Random House.

"The Five W's of Website Evaluation" Kathy Schrock's Guide to Everything. http://www.schrockguide.net/uploads/3/9/2/2/392267/5ws.pdf

Freeman-Loftis, Babs (April 5, 2011) "Morning Routines" Responsive Classroom. Accessed November 24, 2014. https://www.responsiveclassroom.org/ blog/morning-routines.

Leinhardt, G., C. Weidman, and K.M. Hammond (1987) "Introduction and Integration of Classroom Routines by Expert Teachers" *Curriculum Inquiry* 17, no. 2: 135–76.

Linsin, Michael (2009) "Why Routines Make Classroom Management Easier; Plus One Great Idea" Smart Classroom Management. http://www.smartclass-roommanagement.com/2009/11/07/why-routines-make-classroom-manage-ment-easier-plus-one-great-idea/

McLeod, Joyce, and Jan Fisher (2003) *The Key Elements of Classroom Management Managing Time and Space, Student Behavior, and Instructional Strategies*. Alexandria, VA: Association for Supervision and Curriculum Development.

McCloud, Carol, and David Messing (2006) *Have You Filled a Bucket Today?: A Guide to Daily Happiness for Kids*. Northville, MI: Nelson Publishing and Marketing.

Medina, John (2008) *Brain Rules: 12 Principles for Surviving and Thriving at Work, Home, and School*. Seattle, WA: Pear Press.

Pinnell, G.S., and A.M. Jagger (2003) "Oral Language: Speaking and Listening in Elementary Classrooms" in *Handbook of Research on Teaching the English Language Arts*, 2nd ed. Mahwah, NJ: Erlbaum.

Rosenblatt, L.M. (1991) "Literature SOS" *Language Arts* 68, no. 7: 444–48.

Schwartz, S. H. (2012) *An Overview of the Schwartz Theory of Basic Values*. Online Readings in Psychology and Culture, 2(1). http://dx.doi.org/10.9707/2307-0919.1116

Small, Ruth and Marilyn Arnone (2013) WebCheck: The Website Evaluation Instrument. http://www.mywebcheck.net/

Stevens, Robert J., Robert E. Slavin, and Baltimore Students (1992) *The Cooperative Elementary School Effects on Students' Achievement, Attitudes and Social Relations*. Washington, D.C.: ERIC Clearinghouse.

Stronge, James H., and Pamela D. Tucker (2004) *Handbook for Qualities of Effective Teachers*. Alexandria, VA: Association for Supervision and Curriculum Development.

Vallecorsa, Ada, and Laurie Ungerleider DeBettencourt (2000) *Students with Mild Disabilities in General Education Settings: A Guide for Special Educators*. Upper Saddle River, N.J.: Merrill.

Via Institute on Character "Character Strengths Development. http://www.viacharacter.org/www/

Wiggins, Grant P., and Jay McTighe (2005) *Understanding by Design*. Expanded 2nd ed. Alexandria, VA: Association for Supervision and Curriculum Development.

Willis, Judy (2006) *Research-based Strategies to Ignite Student Learning Insights from a Neurologist and Classroom Teacher*. Alexandria, VA: Association for Supervision and Curriculum Development.

Recommended Resources

Adventures of Cyberbee. http://www.mywebcheck.net/

Baskwill, Jane (2013) *Attention-grabbing Tools for Involving Parents in Their Children's Learning*. Markham, ON: Pembroke.

Brain Pickings RSS. Accessed November 24, 2014. http://www.brainpickings.org/.

"Brain-Friendly Teaching (1): Putting Brain-Friendly Strategies To Work" Education World. Accessed November 24, 2014. http://www.educationworld.com/a_curr/profdev/profdev156b.shtml.

Burden, Paul R (2003) *Classroom Management: Creating a Successful K–12 Learning Community*. 2nd ed. New York, NY: Wiley.

Case, Roland (2014) *Active Citizenship: Student Action Projects: A Framework for Elementary and Secondary Teachers to Help Students Plan and Implement Responsible Social Action*. Richmond, BC: RichThinking Resources.

Charlton, Beth Critchley (2005) *Informal Assessment Strategies: Asking Questions, Observing Students and Planning Lessons that Promote Successful Interaction with Text*. Markham, ON: Pembroke Publishers.

"Classroom Guide: Top Ten Tips for Assessing Project-Based Learning" Edutopia. http://www.edutopia.org/10-tips-assessment-project-based-learning-resource-guide

"Critical Evaluation of Information" Kathy Schrock's Guide to Everything. http://www.schrockguide.net/uploads/3/9/2/2/392267/5ws.pdf

Dodge, Judith (2009) *25 Quick Formative Assessments for a Differentiated Classroom*. New York, NY: Scholastic. http://store.scholastic.com/content/stores/media/products/samples/21/9780545087421.pdf

English, Robyn, and Sue Dean (2004) *Show Me How to Learn: Key Strategies and Powerful Techniques that Promote Cooperative Learning.* Markham, ON: Pembroke Publishers.

Fleischman, Paul, and Kevin Hawkes (1999) *Weslandia.* Cambridge, MA: Candlewick Press.

"How To End Each Day On The Right Classroom Management Foot" Smart Classroom Management. Accessed November 24, 2014. http://www.smart-classroommanagement.com/2012/02/11/how-to-end-each-day-on-the-right-classroom-management-foot/.

Kahn, Joyce, and Margaret Foster (2013) *Boosting Executive Skills in the Classroom A Practical Guide for Educators*, Auflage ed. New York, NY: John Wiley & Sons.

Levitin, Daniel J. (2014) *The Organized Mind: Thinking Straight in the Age of Information Overload.* New York, NY: Dutton/Penguin.

MediaSmarts. Accessed November 24, 2014. http://mediasmarts.ca/

Paterson, Kathy (2005) *55 Teaching Dilemmas: Ten Powerful Solutions to Almost Any Classroom Challenge.* Markham, ON: Pembroke Publishers.

Paterson, Kathy (2014) *3-minute Motivators: More than 100 Simple Ways to Reach, Teach, and Achieve More than You Ever Imagined.* Markham, ON: Pembroke Publishers.

Paterson, Kathy (2009) *Desperately Seeking Solutions: Helping Students Build Problem-solving Skills to Meet Life's Many Challenges.* Markham, ON: Pembroke Publishers.

Playworks. Accessed November 24, 2014. http://www.playworks.org/.

Pozzi, Francesca (2010) *Techniques for Fostering Collaboration in Online Learning Communities: Theoretical and Practical Perspectives.* Hershey, PA: Information Science Reference.

Queen's Printer for Ontario (2005) "Assessment Strategies" http://eworkshop.on.ca/edu/pdf/Mod21_assessment_strgs.pdf

"Quick Assessments" BC Student Affairs. http://www.bc.edu/content/dam/files/offices/vpsa/pdf/Quick%20Assessment%20Techniques.pdf

Schultz, Katherine (2003) *Listening: A Framework for Teaching Across Differences.* New York, NY: Teachers College Press.

"Spark Your Brain" Sparking Life. Accessed November 24, 2014. http://www.sparkinglife.org/.

"Tc2" The Critical Thinking Consortium. Accessed November 24, 2014. http://tc2.ca/

"The State of Play" RWJF. Accessed November 24, 2014. http://www.rwjf.org/en/research-publications/find-rwjf-research/2010/02/the-state-of-play.html.

Tompkins, Gail E. (2006) *Language Arts Essentials.* Upper Saddle River, NJ: Pearson/Merrill Prentice Hall.

Visible Thinking. Accessed November 24, 2014. http://www.visiblethinkingpz.org/VisibleThinking_html_files/VisibleThinking1.html.

Waterfall, Milde, and Sarah Grusin (1989) *Where's the Me in Museum: Going to Museums with Children.* Arlington, VA: Vandamere Press.

"What Is Executive Function?" National Center for Learning Disabilities. Accessed November 24, 2014. http://www.ncld.org/types-learning-disabilities/executive-function-disorders/what-is-executive-function.

Wisniewski, David (1999) *Tough Cookie.* New York, NY: Lothrop, Lee & Shepard Books.

Acknowledgments

We would like to thank…

Our former students, for always forcing us to shake our routines every year.

Our colleagues, for inspiring us each and every day.

Mary Macchiusi, for believing in us and prompting our path into classroom routines, and Kat Mototsune, for your careful thought, ideas, and placement of text to make our learning richer. Both of you have enabled us to share our passion, and we are so grateful.

Our family and friends, for your patience, support, and care while we rattled away excitedly about teaching and classroom ideas.

All of our contributors. Finding time in the day is challenging, and we appreciate that you dedicated a chunk to discuss your routines with us. Special thanks to Maran Shona, Steph Donovan, Elaine Rowlands, Guillaume Dupre, Tina Jagdeo, Paul Faggion, Adrienne Fisher, Laurie Fraser, Karyn McCormack, Michael Bushy, David Osorio, and Mark Ferley.

Index